CROCHET DESIGNS OF Anne Orr

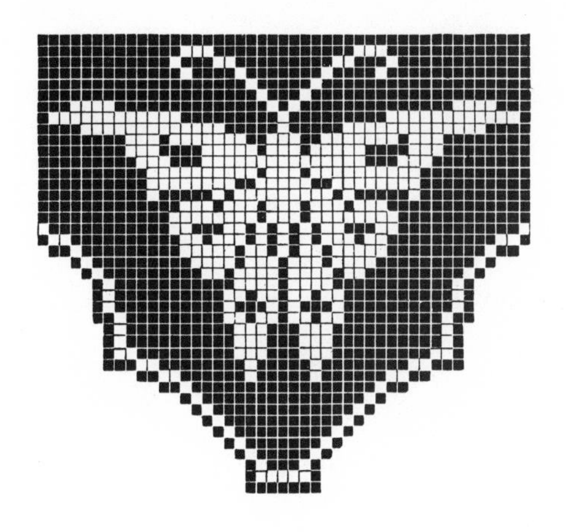

Published through the Cooperation of
THE CENTER FOR THE
HISTORY OF AMERICAN NEEDLEWORK
by
DOVER PUBLICATIONS, INC.
NEW YORK

Published in Canada by General Publishing Company, Ltd., 30 Lesmill Road, Don Mills, Toronto, Ontario.
Published in the United Kingdom by Constable and Company, Ltd., 10 Orange Street, London WC2H 7EG.

This Dover edition, first published in 1978, is a new selection of patterns from *J. & P. Coats, Sweaters, Yokes and Boudoir Caps Crochet Book No. 7,* published by J. & P. Coats, Inc., in 1921; *Anne Orr's Crochet Book of Edgings-Insertions, Corners and Medallions,* published by Anne Orr in 1917; *J. & P. Coats Cross Stitch and Crochet Book No. 9,* published by J. & P. Coats, Inc., in 1922; *J. & P. Coats Crochet, Cross Stitch and Tatting Book No. 14,* published by J. & P. Coats, Inc., in 1923; *J. and P. Coats Little Tots' Articles. Crochet Book No. 6,* published by J. and P. Coats, Inc., in 1920; *J. and P. Coats Crochet Book No. 2,* published by J. and P. Coats, Inc., in 1917; *J. and P. Coats Centerpieces and Edgings, Book No. 16,* published by J. and P. Coats, Inc., in 1923 and *J. & P. Coats Crochet Book of Gown Yokes and Boudoir Caps,* published by J. & P. Coats, Inc., in 1917. A new introduction has been written especially for this edition.

International Standard Book Number: 0-486-23621-8
Library of Congress Catalog Card Number: 77-92502

Manufactured in the United States of America
Dover Publications, Inc.
180 Varick Street
New York, N.Y. 10014

INTRODUCTION

Of the many talented American designers whose needlework patterns began to appear in the first quarter of this century, Anne Champe Orr was certainly among the most prolific and popular. Between 1910 and 1945 Mrs. Orr authored nearly a hundred books of needlework designs in a variety of media including embroidery, crochet, knitting and tatting. Many were published by Mrs. Orr herself from her studio in Nashville, Tennessee; others were done as advertising booklets for thread companies such as Coats and Clark. Originally priced well within the budget of both rural and urban needleworkers, Anne Orr's designs found their way into thousands of American homes, and her books are still collected by many who appreciate the graceful and lively character of her patterns.

Anne Orr herself was a fascinating personality in needlework history. Born at the end of the nineteenth century at a time when the needle arts were flourishing, she studied art in Cincinnati, Chicago and New York before beginning her career with Coats and Clark. By 1915, the young Anne Champe's charted patterns were being featured in color centerfolds of the thread manufacturer's pamphlets and by the end of the 'teens, her name appeared on the covers as principal editor and designer. In 1919, several years after her marriage to wholesale merchant J. Hunter Orr, she joined the staff of *Good Housekeeping* as needlework editor and gained such a following among the magazine's readership that she continues to receive mail addressed to her at the publication's New York office, many years after her death.

Professional accomplishments encompassed only a few of Anne Orr's interests. She was also a contributing member of several women's and community groups and religious organizations, including the prestigious Centennial Woman's and Query clubs and served as director of the Board of the Old Woman's Home of her native Nashville. Mother of three daughters, she also found time in addition to family and career responsibilities to collect old miniatures and to engage in her favorite recreational pastime: driving her own car. Anne Orr's life represents an intriguing blend of traditional and modern womanhood in a time when women's roles were changing almost as rapidly as they are today.

Charted patterns were Mrs. Orr's favorite medium, especially graphed designs for alphabets, flowers, animals and children in engaging costumes and poses. She also borrowed extensively from ethnic needlework, especially Irish crochet and the elegant geometry of East European counted-thread embroidery. Although many of the garments and household articles in this collection may seem fanciful to modern tastes, their vitality and sophistication lend themselves to current applications by a new generation of needleworkers. Anne Orr's dainty centerpieces, table runners and doilies would not only look lovely in a modern home furnished with traditional decor, but the designs are also suitable for pillow tops, other household linens and clothing decoration. The lingerie yokes originally intended for corset covers, camisoles and nightgowns are ideal for summer dresses and tops as well as the "peasant" look blouses and shirts. Her handworked lingerie and crocheted collars and cuffs still retain their feminine appeal.

Although Anne Orr's books were widely distributed during her lifetime, finding acceptance among needleworkers in India, China, France and Spain as well as the United States and Britain, they are now relatively scarce. The present volume is intended as a representative sampling of Anne Orr's work in crochet; her charted designs will be published separately in the Dover Needlework Series. The Center for the History of American Needlework is most grateful to Dover for this opportunity to make Anne Orr's patterns once again available to needleworkers and to honor her achievement in the continuing heritage of American design.

RACHEL MAINES, *President*
Center for the History of American Needlework
Pittsburgh, Pennsylvania

June, 1977

Foundation Stitches and How to Make Them

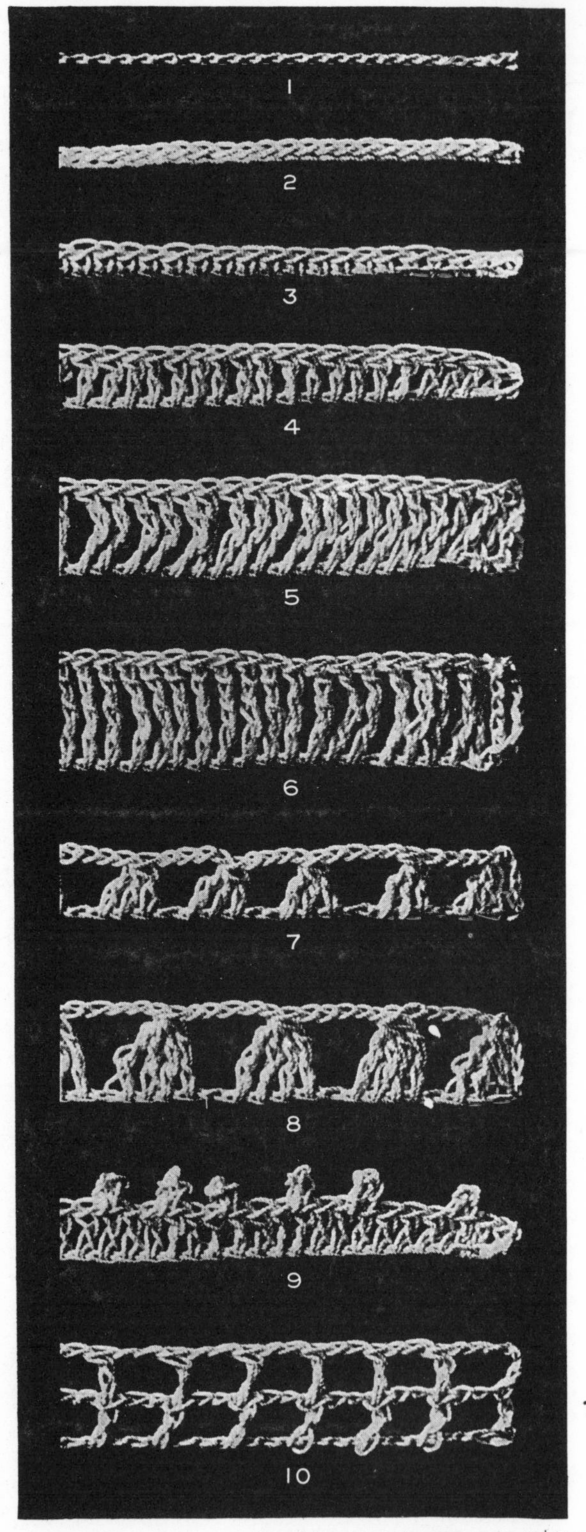

1. CHAIN STITCH (ch)—Is the foundation of all crochet work. Begin by twisting the thread around the needle once, to form a loop, then * throw the thread around the needle and draw through the loop. This forms one chain and is repeated from * for the count or length desired.

2. SLIP STITCH (sl st)—Is most frequently used to join rows, or to slip invisibly from one part of the work to another. Having one loop on the needle, insert the needle in the stitch directed, draw the working thread through this stitch and the loop or the needle with one motion, thus making a flat, close stitch.

3. SINGLE STITCH (s st)—Having one loop on the needle, insert the needle in the stitch directed, draw the working thread through this stitch, making two on the needle, then draw the working thread through these two loops.

4. TREBLE CROCHET (tr)—Having one loop on the needle, throw thread around the needle, insert the needle in the stitch directed, draw working thread through this stitch, making three loops on needle, draw working thread through two loops and then through the remaining two loops. Three chains equal one treble in measure and in count.

5. DOUBLE TREBLE CROCHET (dtr)—Is made similarly to the treble, the difference being that the thread is thrown around the needle twice and the loops are worked off two at a time for three repeats.

6. TRIPLE TREBLE CROCHET (tr tr)—Has the thread thrown around the needle three times and the loops are worked off two at a time for four repeats.

7. HALF TREBLE CROCHET (h tr)—Is sometimes called "group stitch." Having a loop on the needle, throw thread over, insert needle in stitch directed, draw working thread through, draw through two loops, leaving two loops on needle, * thread over, needle in next stitch, draw thread through, draw through two loops, leaving three loops on needle, repeat from *, leaving four loops on needle, then draw thread through all four loops.

8. HALF DOUBLE TREBLE (h d tr)—Is made in the same manner, leaving the last operation of each double treble until the required number have been made and then taking off all the stiches at once.

9. PICOTS (p)—Are usually made by a chain of three or five, then a slip stitch in the first chain. When there is a variation of the above, it is specifically given in the directions.

10. SPACES (sp)—Are the open meshes of filet crochet. To form a space, make one treble, then chain two, skip two stitches of previous row and make another treble. This should result in a perfect square but perfection requires persistent practice as well as the correct sizes of needle and thread. For a space at the beginning of a row, chain five, which allows three for the treble on the edge, and two for the usual chain, two at top of space.

NEW METHOD OF ADDING MESHES AT LAST END OF ROW

All workers know it to be a simple process to increase the length of a row by adding meshes at the first end by making a chain on the end of the preceding row and making the extra blocks or spaces on that chain, but it has been claimed the only way to add meshes at the end of a row already made was to make the trebles run crosswise of the work, which is never very satisfactory as it will look different from the remainder of the row. By using the following method it will all be the same: When making a row on which meshes are to be added at last end of row, instead of making the last treble of the block already there, ch 2, and fasten with a slip stitch to the same loop that ordinarily you would put the last treble in; that will bring your thread even with the lower edge of row, then make a chain long enough to work the extra meshes on. If 1 mesh is required it will want ch of 6; if 2 meshes, ch 9; if 3 meshes, ch 12, adding three stitches for each mesh after the first one; turn and make either sp. or bl. along chain, just which is desired, then fasten with slip stitch to top of last mesh before the chain was added; turn, slip stitch to end of added meshes, then you will be ready to start another row.

Foundation Stitches and How to Make Them

11. BLOCKS (bl)—Are formed by working trebles in adjoining stitches for the required number. Where blocks are consecutive there are four trebles in the first block and three trebles in each following block. Therefore, to find the number of trebles in a row of blocks, multiply the number of blocks by three and add one; in two blocks there are seven trebles, in three blocks, ten trebles, etc.

12. BLOCKS AND SPACES—This illustration clearly shows the alternation of blocks and spaces in filet crochet. Counting from the right to left, as the work is made, there are one block, two spaces, three blocks, one space. The next series of blocks is cut off. This would read in directions, 1 bl, 2 sp, 3 bl, 1 sp.

13. LACET STITCH—Made a foundation chain. **1st Row**—Allow three chains for edge treble, two for two chains and two more for two skipped stitches, work a single stitch in the next chain, * ch 2, skip 2, tr in next, ch 2, sk 2, s st in next. Repeat from * for row.

2d Row—Ch 3 for edge tr, ch 5 more, then tr in tr. * ch, 5, tr in tr. Repeat from * for row. Repeat these two rows for the pattern.

14. KNOT STITCH (k st)—Variously known as Hail Stone or True Lovers' Knot, is made thus: Having one loop on the needle, draw it out to the length of 3 ch, thread over the needle and draw through, making an ordinary chain stich, drawn out to three times its normal length. Then put the needle under than one of the 3 threads of the long loop which seems to lie by itself, draw the thread through and make a single stitch. This is the knot stitch. It is usually worked by making two, then fastening to the previous row by a single stitch unless the row was knot stitch, in which case, work one single stitch each side of the single stitch between the two long loops or knot stitches.

15. LATTICE STITCH (lat st)—Is combination of single knot stitches and trebles. Work a chain, then make one knot stitch, allow three chains for the first treble, and three for the skipped stitches, work a tr in next ch, * one knot stitch, sk 3 ch, 1 tr. Repeat for length desired. This row is repeated for the pattern, working the tr in tr, each time, bringing the knot stitches over each other.

16. SHELL (sh)—May be worked with tr, d tr, or longer, stitches. They are made up of a given number of stitches on each half, separated by a given number of chain stitches. When worked on a foundation chain, a given number of stitches are skipped. When worked over another row of shells, each one is placed in the chain between the halves of the previous shell, or between two shells. In the illustration, the directions would be as follows: Having a chain, allow 3 for the first tr, two tr in 4th chain from needle, ch 2, 3 tr in same chain as last tr, * skip 5 ch, in 6th ch work, 3 tr, 2 ch, and 3 tr. Repeat from * across row. Ch 3 and turn at end of row. Second and all other rows, shell in shell.

11
12
13
14
15
16

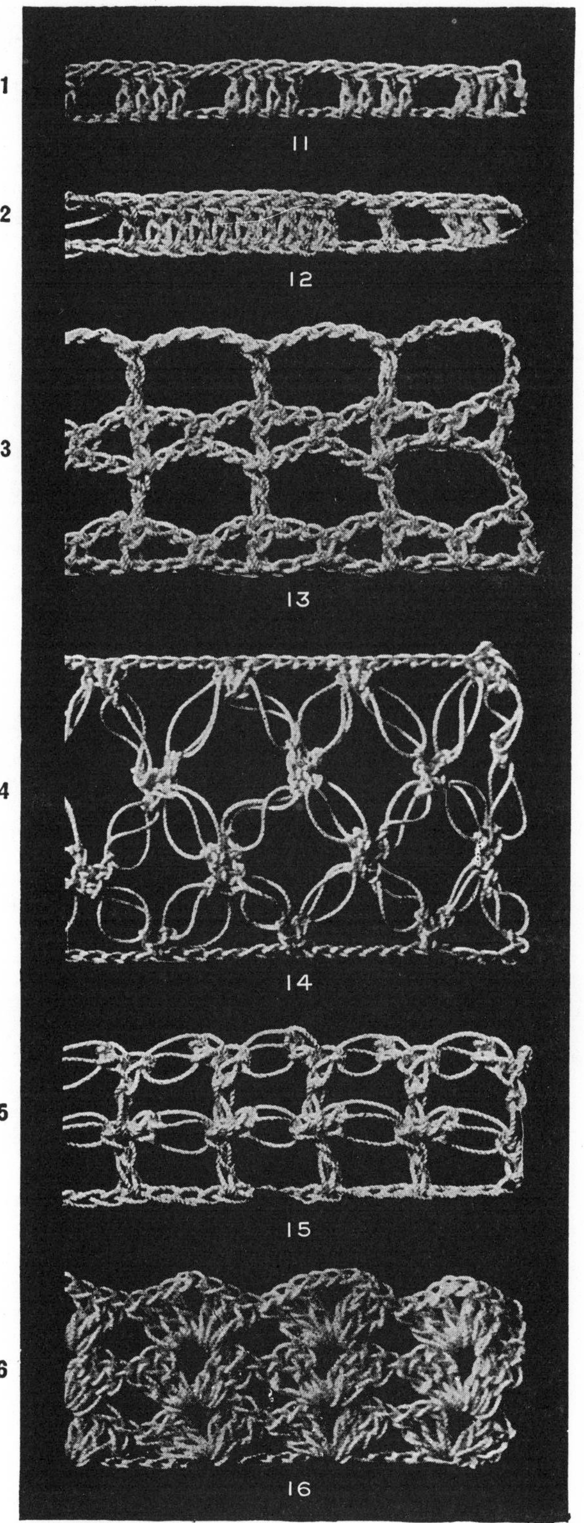

DIRECTIONS FOR FILET CROCHET WORK

The tighter the thread is held, the firmer and more even the work, and if crocheted closely, the following table can be relied upon. However, practice alone will enable the worker to crochet tightly enough to follow this table, and if the thread is loosely held, the meshes will increase to the inch.

The more closely the table is followed, the more beautiful the finished article.

TABLE

Size of Thread	No. Hook	No. of Meshes to the Inch	Size of Thread	No. Hook	No. of Meshes to the Inch	Size of Thread	No. Hook	No. of Meshes to the Inch	Size of Thread	No. Hook	No. of Meshes to the Inch
3	8	3	20	8	5	60	12	7	100	14	..
5	2	3	20 to 30	10	5	70	12	8	100	14	9½ to 10
5	9	4	40	11	6	80	13	8½	If very tight will make 11 meshes to inch.		
10	10	4½	50	12	6½	80	14	9			

Working Patterns for Layette Straps, Towels and Sheets

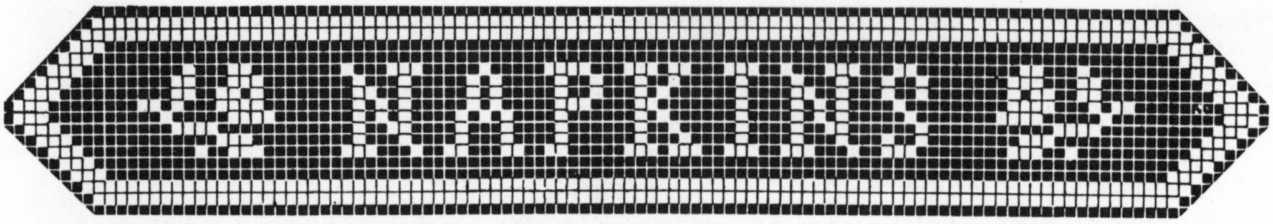

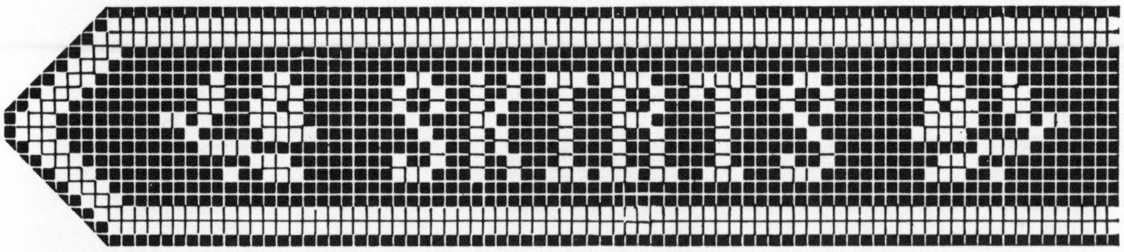

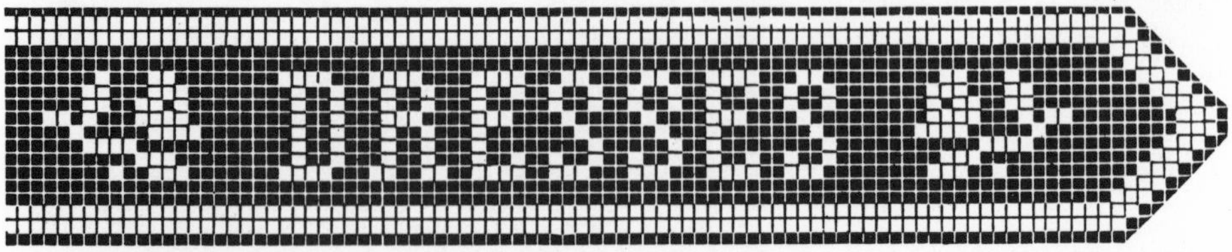

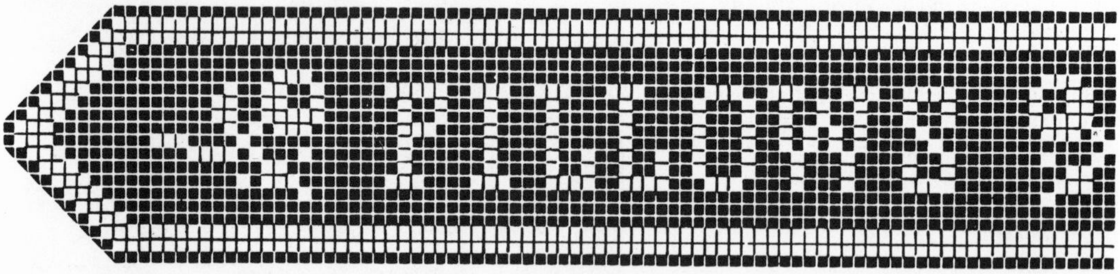

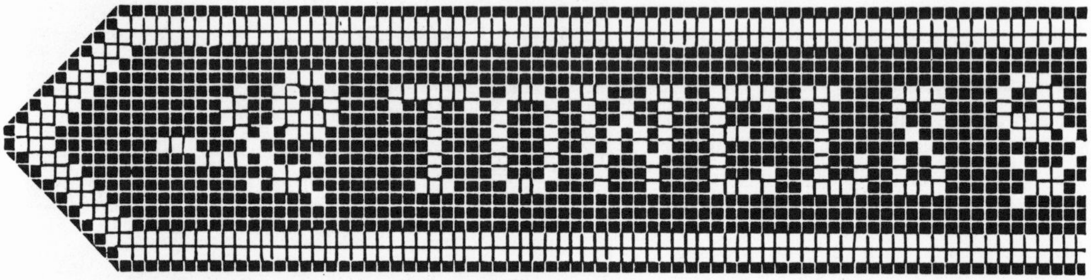

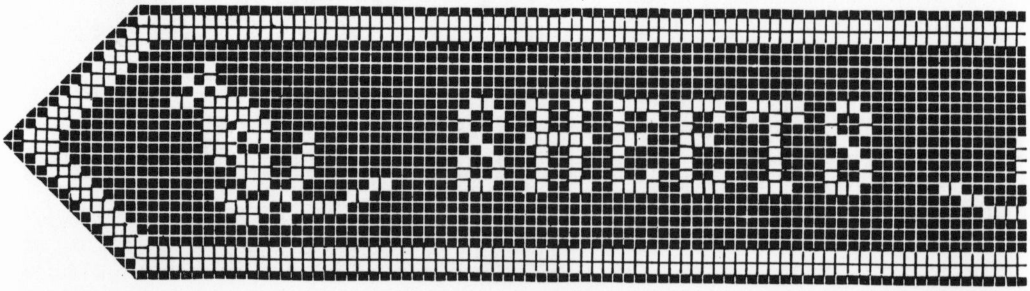

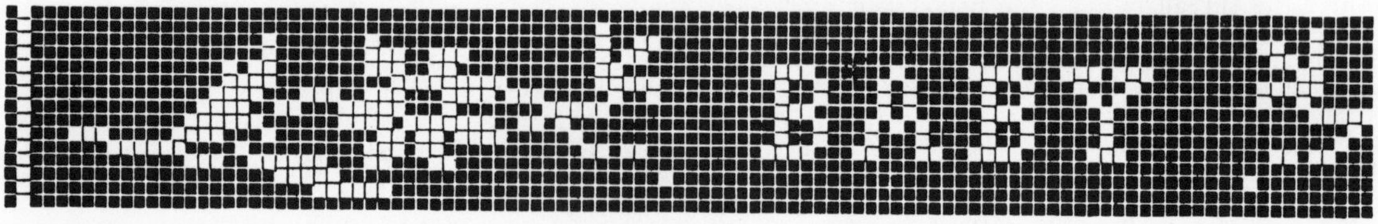

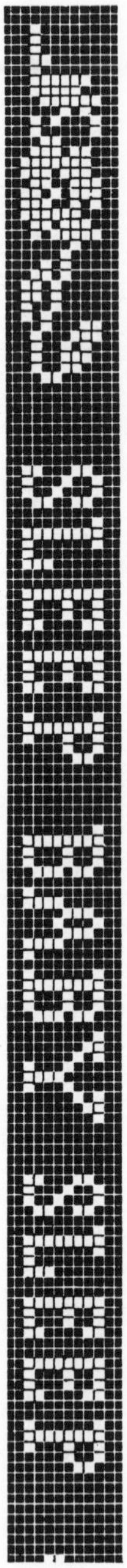

SHEET—INSERT

Layette Straps and Towels

DIRECTIONS FOR LAYETTE STRAPS

Working Pattern on Page 6.

MATERIALS—Coats Mercerized Crochet No. 80. No. 14 Hook.

Ch 11.

1st Row—2 sp.

2d Row—Add sp at each end, 1 sp, 2 bl, 1 sp.

Continue to add 1 sp at each end until it is wide enough, as shown in design.

Follow design and narrow to a point at the last end, making both ends alike.

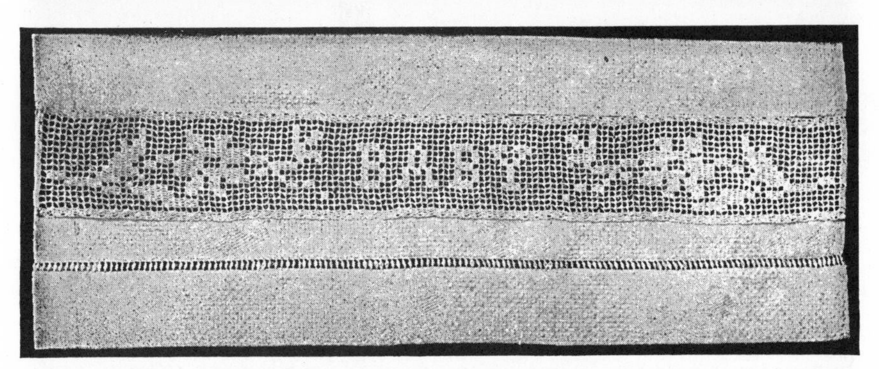

DIRECTIONS FOR TOWEL INSERTION (Baby)

Working Pattern on Page 6.

MATERIALS—Coats Mercerized Crochet No. 80. No. 14 Hook.

Ch 54.

1st Row—17 bl.

2d Row—1 bl, 15 sp, 1 bl.

3d Row—1 bl, 5 sp, 1 bl, 9 sp, 1 bl.

Continue to follow design.

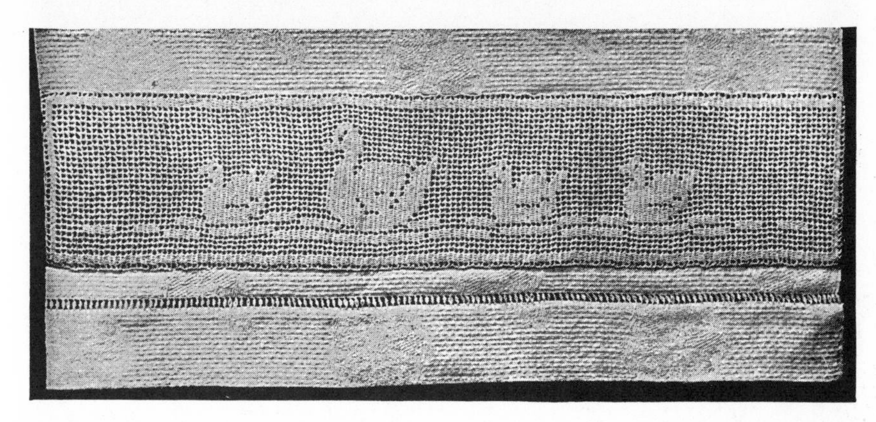

DIRECTIONS FOR TOWEL INSERTION (Ducks)

Working Pattern on Page 8.

MATERIALS—Coats Mercerized Crochet No. 80. No. 14 Hook.

Start at one end, working cross-wise.

Ch 95.

1st Row—30 sp.

2d Row—1 sp, 28 bl, 1 sp.

3d, 4th, 5th, 6th and 7th Rows—1 sp, 1 bl, 26 sp, 1 bl, 1 sp.

8th Row—1 sp, 1 bl, 4 sp, 1 bl, 21 sp, 1 bl, 1 sp, follow design.

Add as many small ducks back of the mother duck as the length of linen requires.

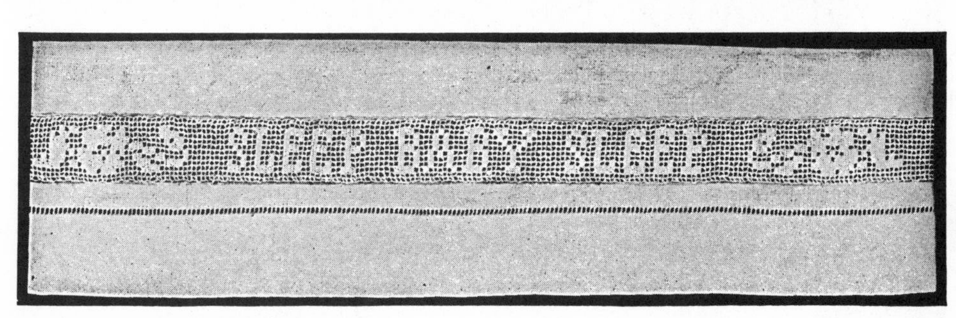

DIRECTIONS FOR SHEET INSERTION (Sleep Baby Sleep)

Working Pattern on Page 6.

MATERIALS—Coats Mercerized Crochet No. 70. No. 14 Hook.

Commence at one end, working cross-wise.

Ch 41.

First 8 Rows—Each 12 sp.

9th Row—Commence design and follow.

Baby Bootees and Sachet

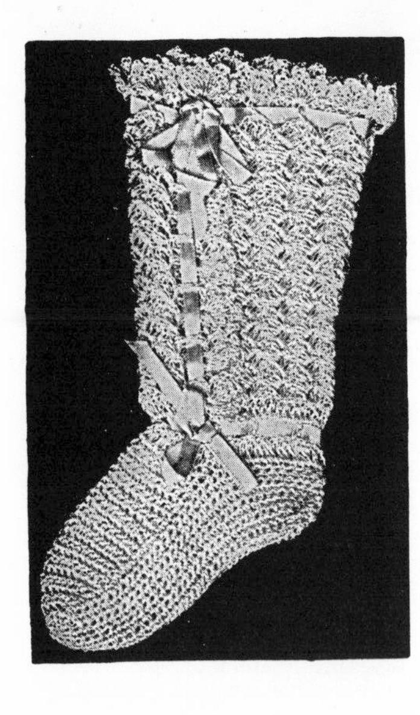

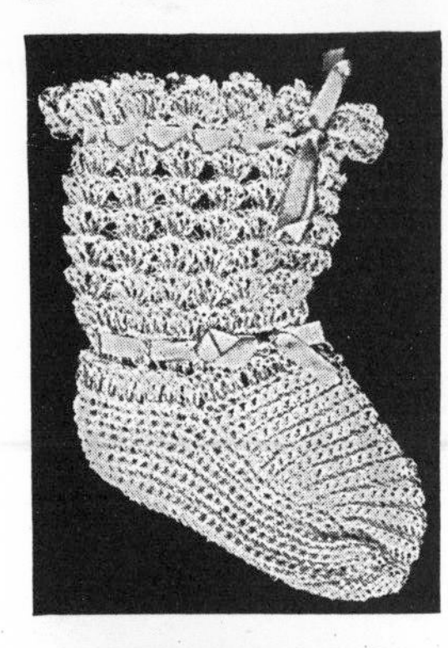

DIRECTIONS FOR BABY SACHET

MATERIALS—Coats Silk Finish Crochet Cotton. No. 8 Hook.

Start at one side, working cross-wise.

Ch 50.

1st Row—Draw up a loop in each of the first 4 st, thread over and draw through the 5 st on hook, ch 1. This makes one star. To make second star, draw a loop through the little hole formed by the st just made, a loop through back of last loop of preceding star and a loop through each of the next 2 st on the ch, thread over and draw through the 5 st on hook, continue to make the stars until there are 24 stars, break cotton and start back at the same end the first row was started.

2d Row—1st star, draw up a loop in two lower ch, in first loop of second star on preceding row in eye of same star, thread over and draw through all five loops. Continue to make stars, leaving off one star at each end of row.

Continue to make each row the same, only leave off one star at each end of each row to form a triangle.

Make another piece like the first triangle, sew together on two sides, stuff with cotton and sachet powder, sew up other side.

EDGE ALL AROUND

Start at corner, * 3 tr in next star, 1 s st in next star. Repeat from *.

DIRECTIONS FOR HIGH TOP BABY BOOTEES

MATERIALS—Coats Silk Finish Crochet Cotton. No. 7 Hook.
Start on top of foot, at toe. Ch 12.
1st Row—11 sc.
2d Row—Add 1 st at each end, 13 sc, taking up both loops.
3d Row—Add 1 st at each end, 15 sc.
4th Row—Add 1 st at each end, 17 sc
5th Row—Add 1 st at each end, 19 sc.
6th Row—19 sc. Repeat the 6th row until the piece is 2½ inches long, ch 32.
1st Row of Leg—49 tr.
2d Row—16 sp.
3d Row—49 tr.
4th Row—* 3 tr in 3d st, ch 2, 1 sc in next st. Repeat from *. 3 tr in 3d st, turn.
5th Row—* 3 tr in ch 2, ch 2, 1 sc in same ch. Repeat from *, turn. Repeat the 5th row until the leg is 5 inches long.

EDGE AROUND TOP AND DOWN SIDE

Ch 5, * 1 tr in 3d st, ch 2. Repeat from *.
2d Row—* 2 tr in 2d tr, 1 p, 2 tr in same tr, 1 p, 2 tr in same tr, 1 p, 2 tr in same tr, 1 s st in next 3. Repeat from *. Sew together up the side.

SOLE

Along half of the lower edge make 33 sc, repeat the row of 33 sc till there are 5 rows. Continue to make 5 rows more, decreasing 1 st on the heel end, break cotton. Make the second half of sole like the first half and sew up in the center of sole.

DIRECTIONS FOR SMALL BABY BOOTEES

MATERIALS—Coats Silk Finish Cotton. No. 7 Hook.
Start at toe on top of foot. Ch 12.
1st Row—10 s st.
2d Row—Increase 1 st at each end, 12 s st, take each st in back loop to form ridges.
3d Row—Increase 1 st at each end, 14 s st.
4th Row—Increase 1 st at each end, 16 s st.
5th Row—Increase 1 st at each end, 18 s st.
6th Row—Increase 1 st at each end, 20 s st.
7th Row—20 s st. Repeat the 7th row until there are 12 ridges, ch 30, join to the other side for the ankle.
1st Row—1 tr in each st all around.
2d Row—Ch 5, * 1 tr in 3d st, ch 2. Repeat from * all around.
3d Row—* 1 tr over tr, 2 tr in sp. Repeat from *.
4th Row—Ch 3, 1 tr in 1st st, ch 1, 2 tr in same st, * 2 tr in 4th st, ch 1, 2 tr in same st. Repeat from *.
5th Row—2 tr in ch 1, ch 1, 2 tr in same ch. Repeat all around.
6th, 7th, 8th and 9th Rows—Like 5th row.
10th Row—Ch 5, * 1 tr in ch 1, ch 2, 1 tr between shells, ch 2. Repeat from *.
11th Row—6 tr in tr, * sk 1 tr, 6 tr in next tr. Repeat from *.
12th Row—(Ch 2, 1 sl st in top of tr) 5 times, ch 4, 1 sl st in top of tr in 10th row, ch 4, 1 sl st in top of tr. Repeat.

SOLE

Along one-half of the lower edge make 30 s st, for the first row. Make 5 more rows like the 1st row. Next 5 rows leave off one st on each row on the end where the heel is. Make the other side of sole like the first half and sew up in the center of sole.

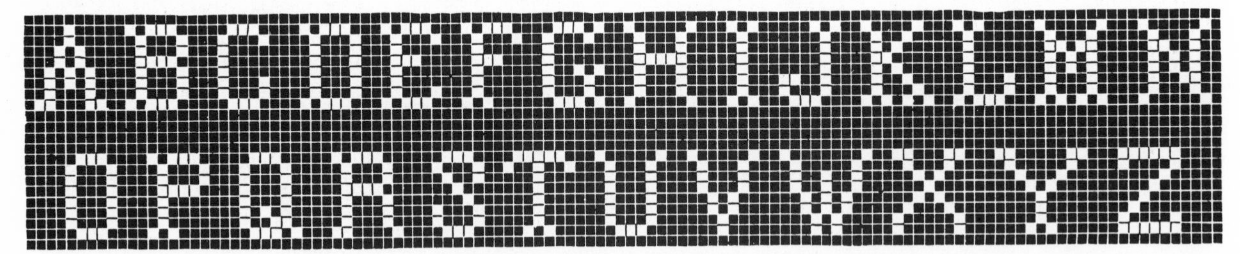

USEFUL ALPHABET FOR BABY

Belgian Baby Cap

DIRECTIONS FOR BELGIAN BABY CAP

MATERIALS—Coats Mercerized Crochet No. 100. No. 14 Hook.

Make 10 meshes to inch.

CROWN

Start at front, working cross-wise.

Ch 348.

1st Row—115 bl.

Next 5 Rows—1 bl, 113 sp, 1 bl.

7th Row—Start the flowers and follow design, leaving off meshes at each side to form the oval shape as shown in design.

EDGE ALL AROUND

Start at one end, working cross-wise.

Ch 63.

1st Row—1 bl, 18 sp, 1 bl.

2d Row—Add 1 bl at lower edge, 1 bl, 1 sp, 1 bl, 4 sp, 1 bl, 12 sp, 1 bl. Continue to follow design, adding bl at lower edge to form scallop. Make edge long enough to go all around crown, which if 10 to inch requires 2 corners and 13 scallops, plain, across front of cap and joined to this across bottom of crown are 28 scallops, sewed to the side of front edge corner and fulled on. A narrow ribbon sewed to lining of cap where insertion at back joins the corner, is used for beading through which to run narrower ribbon to tie and full the crown at back of neck.

Fancy rosettes to hold strings complete a beautiful cap.

Things for Baby's Wear

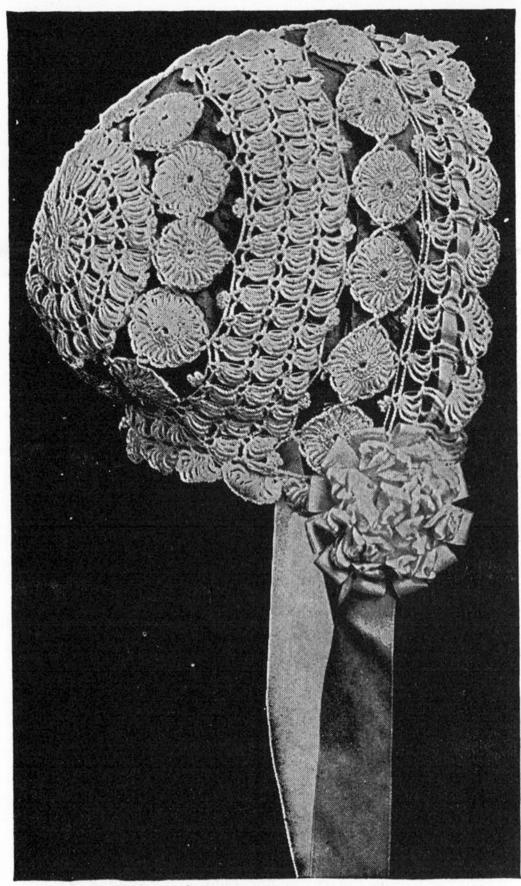

DIRECTIONS FOR BABY CAP
(Roll Stitch)

MATERIALS—Coats Mercerized Crochet No. 30. No. 12 Hook.

Start in center of crown, working around.

Ch 10, join.

1st Row—16 tr in ring, join.

2d Row—25 roll st in the 16 tr, join.

(Roll Stitch is made as follows—Wrap the cotton around needle 20 times, insert hook in stitch on last row, thread over, draw through 1st thread over, draw through all the stitches on needle, thread over, draw through 1st.)

3d Row—Ch 9, 1 tr in same place, * ch 3, 1 tr after 2d roll, ch 2, 1 tr in same place. Repeat from *, join.

4th Row—4 roll st in * ch 2, ch 2, 4 roll st in next ch 2. Repeat from *, join.

5th Row—Like the 3d row.

6th Row—Like the 4th row.

7th Row—Start in center of group of 4 roll st, * ch 7, 1 sl st in center of next group of 4, ch 5, 1 sl st in same place, ch 7, 1 sl st in same place, ch 5, 1 sl st in same place. Repeat from *.

8th Row—Is 11 medallions each. Medallions made as follows—Start in center, ch 6, join.

1st Row—14 tr in ring, join.

2d Row—28 roll st in the 14 tr.

3d Row—Ch 7, 1 sl st after 2d roll st. Repeat all around, break cotton and make another medallion.

9th Row—Start at the middle of edge of medallion, * ch 18, catch in 6th st from hook for sp, ch 7, 1 sl st in same place, ch 5, 1 sl st in same place, ch 12, 1 sl st in top of next medallion. Repeat from *.

10th Row—Ch 5, 1 tr in same place, * ch 6, 1 tr in 5th st of ch, ch 2, 1 tr in same place. Repeat from *.

11th Row—Like the 9th row.

12th Row—Like the 3d row.

13th Row—Like the 4th row, only it does not go across the back of neck.

14th Row—Like the 3d row, only as far as the 13th row next.

15th Row—Like the 9th row.

16th Row—Like the 3d row.

17th Row—Like the 7th row.

18th Row—12 medallions.

19th Row—Like the 10th row.

20th Row—Like the 3d row.

21st Row—Like the 4th row.

22d Row—* 2 roll st in ch 2, ch 6, 1 roll st in center of group of 4 roll st, ch 3. Repeat from *.

23d Row—Runs all around bonnet. Start in 2d roll st, * 10 roll st in ch 6, 1 sl st in top of 2d roll st. Repeat from *.

24th Row—Start in sl st, * ch 6, 1 sl st after 2d roll st. Repeat from .

DIRECTIONS FOR BABY JACKET

MATERIALS—Coats Silk Finish Crochet Cotton. No. 7 Hook.

Start at lower edge of back, working cross-wise.

Ch 156.

1st Row—51 bl.

2d and 3d Rows—51 sp.

4th Row—Start butterflies, follow design. After the 27th row, add a ch of 63 st each side, on which make 20 meshes for sleeves. After the 41st row drop off the 13 center meshes and all one side and work down the other side for one sleeve and one front. After the first front is finished, break cotton and start back at the back of neck. Make the second front like the first one. Sew up sleeves and under arms

EDGE ALL AROUND

Start in bl, * (ch 4, 1 sl st in next bl), 4 times, ch 5, 1 sl st in same place, ch 7, 1 sl st in same place, ch 5, 1 sl st in same place. Repeat from *.

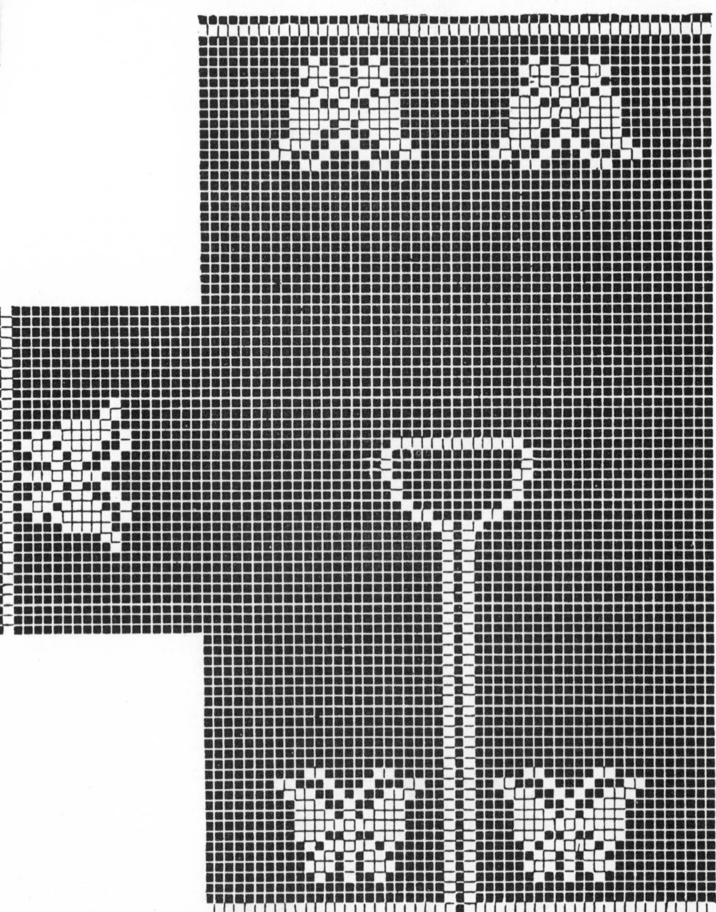

WORKING PATTERN FOR JACKET

Baby Carriage Robe

DIRECTIONS FOR BABY CARRIAGE ROBE

MATERIALS—Coats Mercerized Crochet No. 80, with No. 12 needle.

This is made in squares. 12 little rings in first and last squares. 8 in the rest of rows. The first ring is started with a ch of 9, all the others with 12; 8 for the ring, the rest for the ch between rings. In the first ring make 2 sc, p, 2 sc. **2d Ring**—Ch 12, join into 8 st from needle; in this ring 2 sc, p, 2 sc, p, 2 sc. The 3d, 5th, 6th, 8th, 9th, 11th, 12th are all made like the 2d. The 4th, 7th, and 10th are made like the 1st except they commence with 12 ch. When 12 rings are made join with 3 ch to 1st st of 1st ring, being careful that all the ch loops are untwisted and that the picots are all in the inside of the square. On the outside ch 3 and go back, beginning with the 2d ring made. Make rings 2, 3, 5, 6, 8, 9 with 3 p on the outside, like the inside. Rings 4, 7 are made 2 sc, p, 2 sc, p, 2 sc, p, 2 sc, p, 2 sc, making 3 ch between all rings. When the 9th ring is finished, ch 3, 2 sc, p, 2 sc into the 10th ring at the corner, then start another square with 12 ch, making rings 2, 3, 4, 5, 6, 7, 8, 9 as you did the first, joining the 9th to the side of the 7th ring of the 1st square. Ch 3 and turn, finishing five of these rings as you did the first ten. Make 22 squares like this, leaving one side unfinished. When the 22 are done, go back and make the bottom clear across, making 3 ch between rings, and 3 p in each ring as before. For the star ch 8, join, ch 6, fasten in center p of a ring on inside of square. On this ch 6, make 1 sc, 4 tr, join to ring in center. Make 8 of these points, fastening two on each side of the square.

Design for Use in the Nursery

Baby Afghan

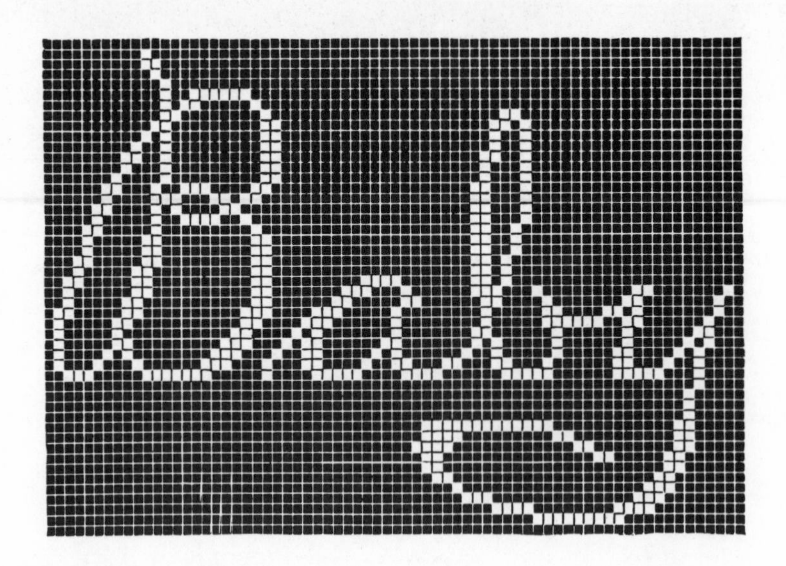

DIRECTIONS FOR BABY AFGHAN

MATERIALS—Coats Pearl Cotton No. 5, No. 2 Hook and an Afghan Hook.

Ch 147 with afghan hook.

1st Row—Make the afghan stitch as on page 15 and continue to make until robe is 30 in. long.

BEADING—Use No. 2 hook.

1st Ro w—Make a row of sps all around robe.

2nd Row—Ch 10, *thread over hook 5 times, put hook in the top of the next tr of last row, pull thread through, work off by twos all the sts on needle except last two, thread over hook 5 times, put hook in same st as last time, pull thread through, work off the sts except the last two, thread over hook 5 times, put hook in same st as before, pull thread through, work off the sts except the last three, there will be 4 sts on hook, thread over, draw through these 4, ch 2, thread over hook 5 times, put needle in top of next tr of last row, draw thread through, work off by twos all the sts on hook, ch 2, repeat from *.

EDGE—Fasten thread in the top of st that was thrown 5 times over hook, * 1 s st in same st, 2 tr in 1st st of ch 2, 2 d tr and 2 tr tr in next st of ch, sl st down last tr tr to last row, sl st on last row to the top of st that was thrown 5 times over hook, repeat from *.

DIRECTIONS FOR CROSS-STITCH OF PILLOW AND AFGHAN

Cross-stitch pillow from colored chart on plate 2, on canvas 12 squares to the inch, of Coats Six Strand Floss, (using four strands to this size canvas,) using Light Pink 3, Beauty Pink 65 and Rose 46 for the flowers, and Moss Green 5 and Dk Moss Green 60 for the leaves.

The Afghan is cross-stitched with 6 strands of Coats Six Strand Floss, right over the squares made of the afghan stitch, with same colors as used on the pillow, following the designs on plate 2, with additional Light Blue 7 and Blue 8 for the bow knots and letters.

Baby Afghan and Pillow

Counterpane with Crochet and Cross-Stitch

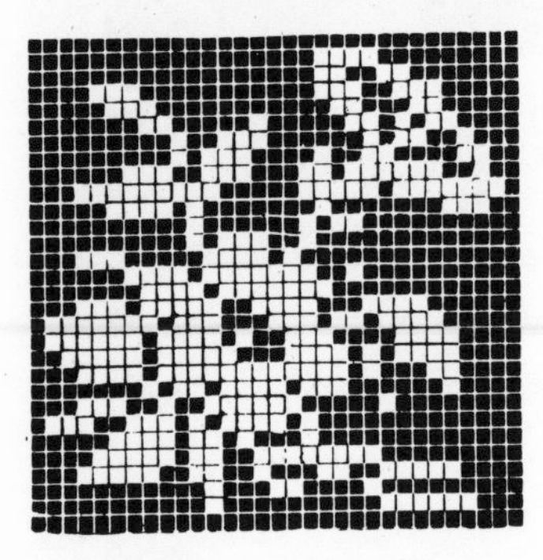

DIRECTIONS FOR CROCHET COUNTERPANE

Filet Strip

Materials—Coats Pearl Cotton No. 8. No. 7 Hook.
6 meshes to the inch.
Start at one end, working cross-wise.
Ch 198
1st Row—65 bl.
2nd, 3rd and 4th Rows—Each 65 sp.
5th Row—Start flowers and follow design.

Center Strip

Materials—Coats Pearl Cotton No. 3 and bone afghan hook.
Ch 121 and proceed as the directions for afghan stitch.

Edge Strip

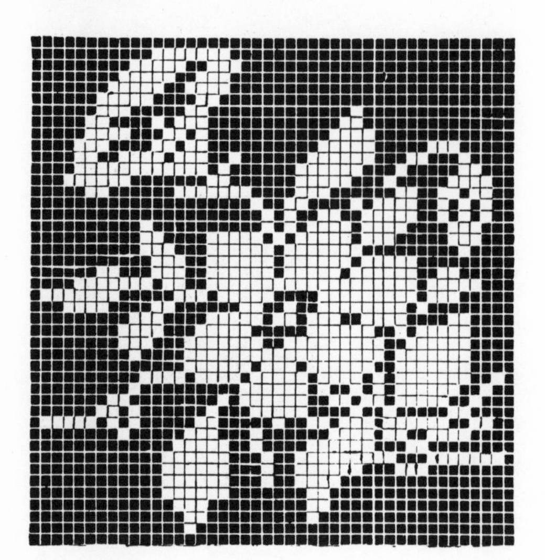

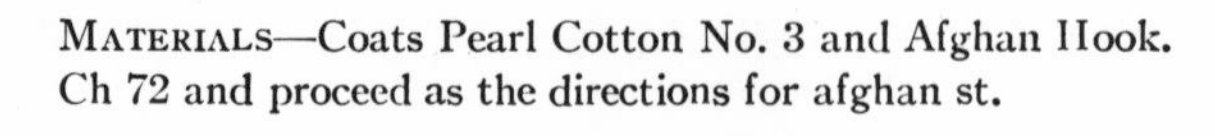

Materials—Coats Pearl Cotton No. 3 and Afghan Hook.
Ch 72 and proceed as the directions for afghan st.

Border

Materials—Coats Pearl Cotton No. 3.
Make two rows of sps of filet.

Fringe

Wind No. 3 Coats Pearl Cotton over a card-board large enough so ends when cut will be 22 inches long, take 6 pieces, fold in center and with crochet hook loop the piece in sp, continue to put 6 pieces in each sp. To tie the fringe, take half of one group and half of the next group and tie together with one knot, continue all around. To tie the second row, do the same as the first row, tying one half of one group with one half of the next group all around. Lay flat on table and trim fringe even.

This Counterpane all crochetted, is a real heirloom, but if one wants to simplify the work, use a heavy linen 12 and 18 inches wide for the strips to carry cross-stitch, instead of the afghan stitch.

CROSS-STITCH ON COUNTERPANE

The strips of the crochetted counterpane are cross-stitched right on the square mesh of afghan stitch with 8 strands of floss.

The narrow strips have bunches of flowers worked from the filet pattern shown here, and the flowers are made of different tones, as pleases the worker. The center flower of the sprays have three petals on one side of flower made of Beauty Pink 65 and Rose 46 while the top flower in the sprays are made of one tone, either of Blue 8 with yellow center dots of Yellow 9, or the other of Lavender 30 with same yellow center. Changing the coloring of flowers this way, with each spray added, gives a wonderful effect, and is more interesting to the worker.

The large leaves should be worked in Dark Moss Green 60 and the small leaves and stems in Moss Green 5. The bunch on the large strips should be followed by matching the colors on plate 1 in the design shown for this purpose. This is the purpose of giving the worker the colored patterns to work from.

It requires three large sprays for the wide center strip to complete the counterpane.

If the worker prefers, the cross-stitching can be done on linen strips, measuring 18 inches in width for center strip, and 12 inches for the narrow strips. Cross-stitch on canvas, 8 squares to the inch, as directed.

DIRECTIONS FOR AFGHAN STITCH

Make a ch the desired length, draw up a loop through the horizontal bar in the back of second and all succeeding chain stitches, keeping all loops on hook. This is half the afghan row. Work back as follows; cotton over and through end stitch, * over and through 2 stitches, repeat from * next row, pick up a loop through the 2nd and each succeeding perpendicular bar, keeping all loops on hook. The end st is picked up through the last bar and the thread back of it Repeat last 2 rows till the desired size.

Counterpane with Crochet and Cross-Stitch

Pillow

DIRECTIONS

MATERIALS—J. & P. Coats Mercerized Crochet Cotton, No. 50, for the filet center and No. 30 for the edge.

Ch 350 and work 115 sp for the first row. **2d Row**—1 sp, 113 bl, 1 sp, ch 5, turn. **3d Row**—1 sp, 1 bl, 111 sp, 1 bl, 1 sp, ch 5, turn. The next 8 rows are like the 3d. **12th Row**—1 sp, 1 bl, 52 sp, 7 bl, 52 sp, 1 bl, 1 sp, ch 5, turn. Follow pattern on page 17.

FOR THE EDGE—Use the heavy thread and work a row of sp all around, making 4 tr, separated by 2 ch, in each corner. **2d Row**—* 3 s st in 1st sp; in next sp, 1 s st, picot of 3 ch, 1 s st; in next space, 3 s st. Ch 12, turn, 1 sl st in first s st, ch 1, turn, over the 12 ch work, 6 s st, p, 6 s st, p, 6 s st, sl st into tr, and repeat from * all around.

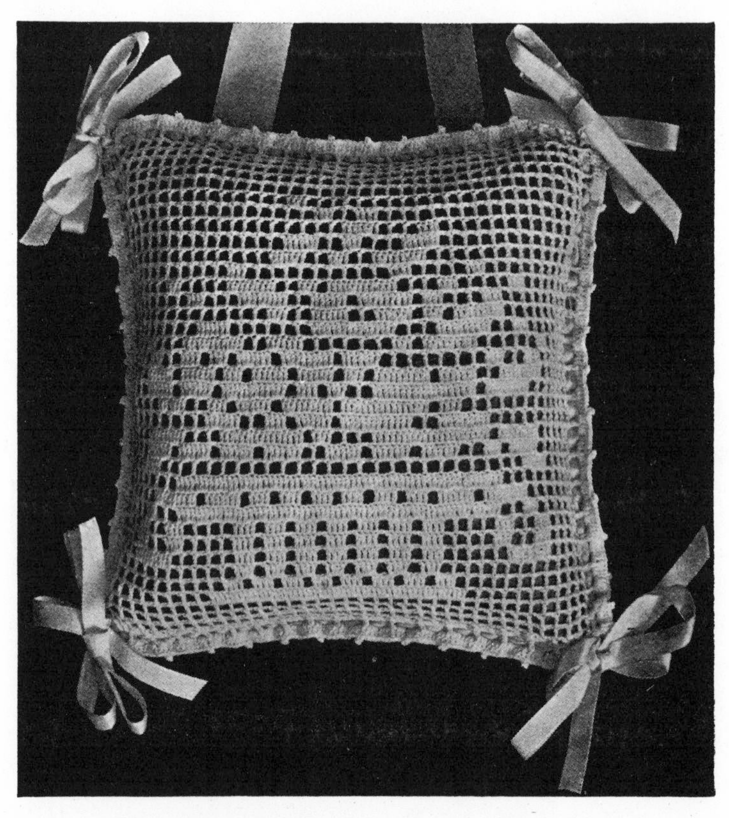

This pincushion is so plain in cut, any worker in filet can copy without directions

Counterpane for Bow Knot Bed Room Set

If made of J. & P. Coats Mercerized Crochet Cotton, No. 30, and tightly done, the medallion as illustrated including border, will measure about 25 inches square. This is to be set in heavy linen, as a center medallion, and another border is made, from this pattern, using a corner and eight single roses to each side, and the second border set about 8 inches from edge of crocheting in center of spread.

The pillow sham should carry through its center a strip of the border in crochet, the width of bed-spread.

The basket of flowers shows a particularly beautiful design for a counterpane center. To make it, with a row of blocks for the outside, ch 343, and make a row of 340 trebles, then 9 rows of 1 bl, 111 sp, 1 bl, ch 3, turn. **11th Row**—1 bl, 52 sp, 7 bl, 52 sp, 1 bl, ch 3, turn. Follow pattern.

The border is attractive for the edge of spread or dresser scarf. Begin at the right side of illustration, allow for 1 block at each side of the border, and ch 121. For 1st, 3d and 5th rows, work 1 bl, 11 sp, 2 bl, 24 sp, 1 bl, ch 3, turn. **2d and 4th Rows**—1 bl, 24 sp, 2 bl, 11 sp, 1 bl, ch 3, turn. **6th Row**—1 bl, 19 sp, 3 bl, 2 sp, 2 bl, 11 sp, 1 bl, ch 3, turn. Follow pattern, working to the extreme edge. Then, to turn the corner, work along the outer 40 meshes of the side, continuing the design as shown.

Bath Rugs

DIRECTIONS FOR ROUND RUG

Materials—Coats Pearl Cotton No. 3, and No. 5 Hook.

Crochet four in a chain, pull through first chain, then pull up thread on hook height of tr crochet, pull through then tr crochet sixteen times, catch through first tr crochet at top, be sure to make up both threads then, draw up thread on needle again, adding two extra tr crochet, or enough to make lay flat, without cupping. Repeat until desired size; always laying down each row to see if it lays flat, neither too full, nor too cuppy.

When desired size is made crochet around twice or three times with s st to give body to rug, or firm edge, also add an extra stitch so it won't roll or curl up.

DIRECTIONS FOR CROSS-STITCH

Cross-stitch over the crochet blocks, following pattern of chart above.

Cross-stitch roses in Rose 46 and stems in Moss Green 5.

DIRECTIONS FOR OVAL RUG

Materials—Coats Pearl Cotton No. 3 White, Coats Pearl Cotton No. 3 Blue, No. 2 Hook.

Start in center and work round and round.

Ch 104.

1 tr in each st of ch, 6 tr in end st of ch, then work back on other side of ch by making 1 tr in each st of ch, continue to work around and around adding enough tr in the end stitches so it will be flat and not hoop.

After 16 rows are made each side of middle, make 5 rows of blue, 5 rows of white, 5 rows of blue, 1 row of white, 1 row of blue, 1 row of blue on edge made with s st instead of tr.

DIRECTIONS FOR CROSS-STITCH

Letters on rug and hot plate mats are made of Blue 8 with dashes of black—by following letters shown on page 19.

HOT PLATE MATS

Japanese Alphabet

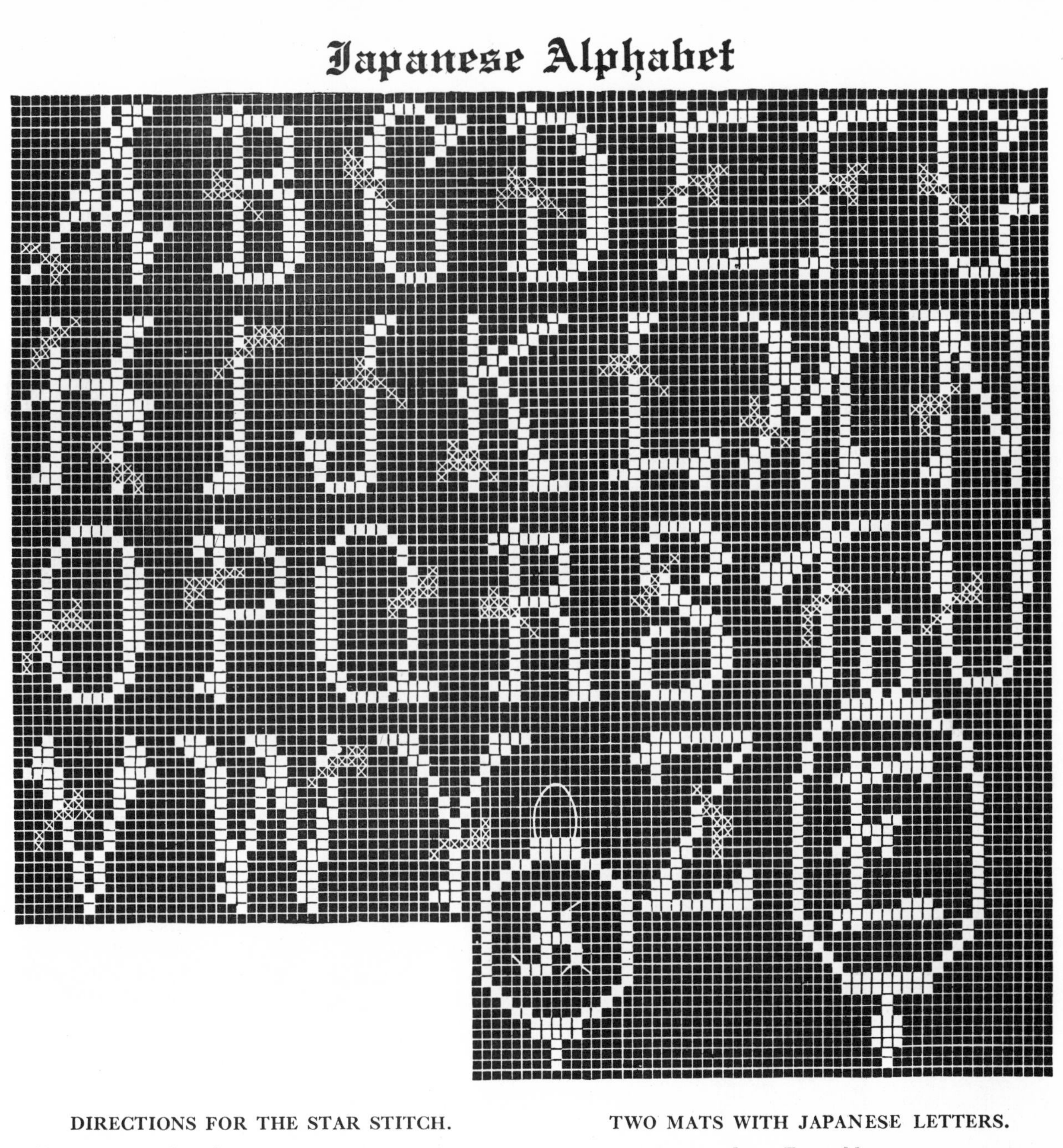

DIRECTIONS FOR THE STAR STITCH.

Ch an even number of sts, turn.

1st Row—Draw up a loop in each of 4 sts, thread over, draw through 5 loops on hook, ch 1, draw loop through eye of preceding star (the little hole formed by the st just made) a loop through back of last loop of preceding star, and a loop through each of next 2 sts on the ch; finish star as before. Continue to work as for 2nd star until row is complete, then fasten thread on wrong side and break off.

2nd Row—Begin at the first side. Make a loop on the hook and catch it in the very edge with a sl st, ch 3, draw up a loop in 2 lower chs in 1st loop in 1st star on preceding row and in eye of same star; finish star as usual. Take up the sts in other stars as follows: eye of preceding star back of last loop of same star, 1st st in star in row below eye of same star.

To widen at beginning of row in star stitch, fasten thread as though it were to be made even, ch 5, take up loops in last 4 sts of ch, finish as usual and proceed as before.

To widen at end of row. At the end of the row before which it is desired to widen ch 3, break thread. In the last star on the next row, draw loops throw 2 sts of the ch 3, and finish as before.

To narrow at beginning of row. Instead of fastening thread in very edge of row, fasten it in the eye of first star and continue as usual.

To narrow at end of row, leave the last star off and fasten thread as usual.

TWO MATS WITH JAPANESE LETTERS.

Long Table Mat.

Materials—Coats Pearl Cotton No. 5, No. 7 Hook and Coats Six Strand Floss in blue and black.

Ch 32.

1st Row—Make 14 Stars.

For the next 11 rows, add a star at beginning and end of row. There will now be 36 stars. Make 31 rows each having 36 stars, narrow 1 star at each end for 11 rows.

Square Table Mat.

Ch 54.

1st Row—Make 25 stars.

For the next 11 rows add 1 star at beginning and end of each row. There will now be 47 stars. Make 25 rows of 47 stars each, narrow 1 star at each end of each row for 11 rows.

Edge Around Mats.

Use 3 strands of Coats Six Strand Floss. Fasten thread in eye of star, *4 tr in eye of next star, ch 3, sl st in top of last tr, 4 tr in same st as last 4 tr, s st in eye of next star, repeat from *.

Make two sides like each mat. Sew the sides together on three sides. Sew snaps on the end that was left open. Cut sheet asbestos the size to fit the mats and enclose in them.

To cross stitch, have stitches running from eye to eye of star and follow alphabet on this page.

Tea Tray

DIRECTIONS

This tea tray measures 11x15 inches.

MATERIALS—J. & P. Coats Mercerized Crochet Cotton, No. 100.

Ch 387 and work 6 rows of 127 spaces each. **7th Row**—Sets the pattern for the letters. 12 sp, 2 bl, 3 sp, 2 bl, 4 sp, 2 bl, 6 sp, 4 bl, 2 sp, 4 bl, 8 sp, 4 bl, 2 sp, 2 bl, 3 sp, 2 bl, 2 sp, 1 bl, 3 sp, 1 bl, 5 sp, 3 bl, 8 sp, 3 bl, 6 sp, 1 bl, 4 sp, 1 bl, 3 sp, 1 bl, 4 sp, 4 bl, 2 sp, 1 bl, 12 sp. Follow the working pattern for remainder of design.

A Most Attractive and Useful Tray for the Afternoon Tea.

WORKING MODEL FOR DESIGN IN TEA TRAY

Leave as many open meshes outside the design, as necessary to fit your frame or tray.

Luncheon Set

APPROPRIATELY DESIGNED IN A VASE OF FLOWERS

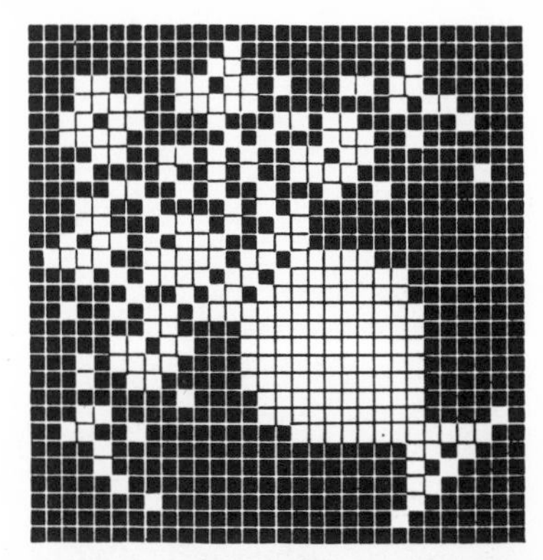

WORKING DESIGN FOR CENTER PIECE

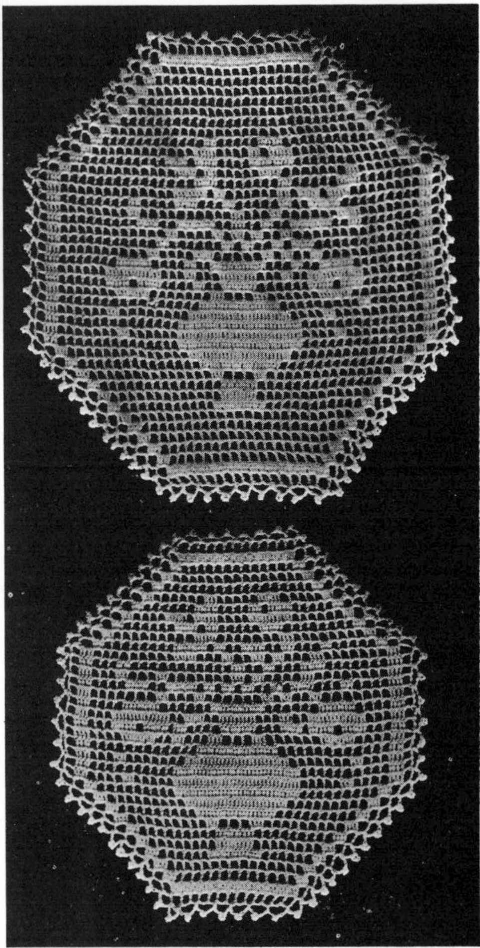

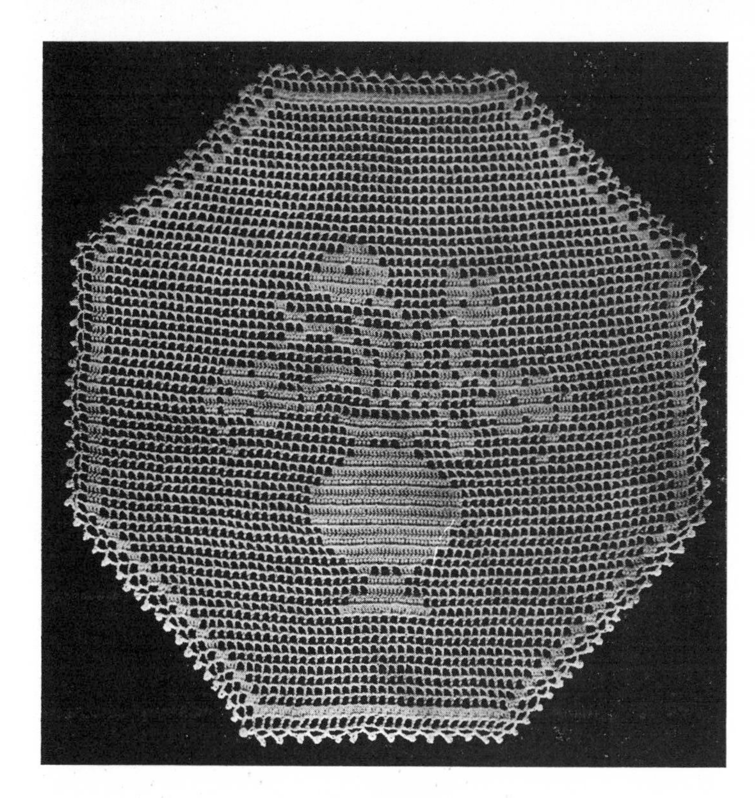

DIRECTIONS

CENTERPIECE WITH FILET POINTS

MATERIALS—7 balls Crochet Cotton No. 50. Linen center 21 in. in diameter.

On this linen turn a hem 1-8 in. wide; over this hem, 1-8 in. apart, put 3 dc. Make the outer edge as close and firm as possible. It must be done with a very fine hook and fine crochet cotton.

2nd Row—Ch 5, * dc in same st, dc in 3d st, ch 2; repeat from *.

3rd Row—Ch 5, dc under ch of 2 in last row, * dc in next ch of 2, ch 2, dc under same ch; repeat from *. For the circle make twelve points. Ch 71, first row. 3 dc in 5th st from needle, 2 dc over 2 dc. 32 sp of 2 ch, sk 1 st, dc in 2 st, repeat 31 times, ch 4, turn. Ch 1, dc over dc—2 dc in small sp at end of row. Ch 4, turn. In this end loop always make 2 dc—both ways. Follow the working model for the pattern.

When you have completed 32 rows, you will have 66 dc, 1 sp (at the upper side) of 1 ch, 1 dc, ch 4, turn. 2 dc in small sp, 2 dc over 2 dc, * ch 2 sk 1 st, dc over dc. * repeat until have 32 sp. When points are all done, make an edge by * ch 2, p ch 2, sk 1 dc, sl st into next dc. * Repeat around.

DOILEY FOR SERVING PLATE

Largest Size—Ch 91, turn, 1 dc in 8th. 1 dc in each st 81 times. Ch 2, sk 2, 1 dc, turn.

2nd Row—Ch 7 dc in last dc of first row, 2 dc in sp, dc in next dc, 27 open meshes over solid meshes of first row, then follow design.

DOILEY FOR BREAD PLATE

Ch 58, proceed same as large size.

GLASS DOILEY

Ch 46, proceed same as large size.

EDGE

Fasten in open sp. * ch 7, fasten with sc in 3d st of ch, ch 3, 1 sc in next sp, repeat from *.

Thoroughly Japanese in Design is this Library Table Runner

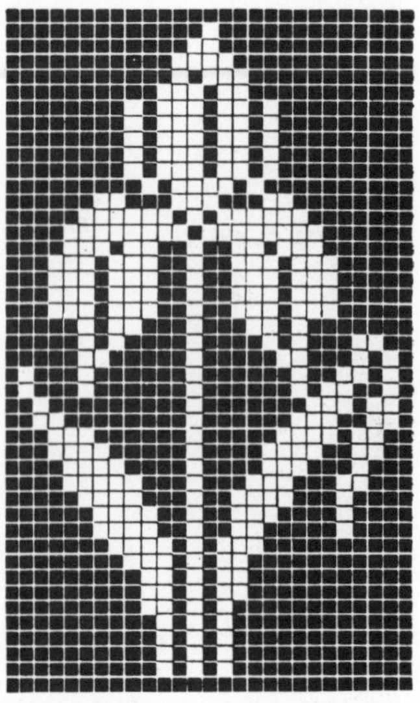

Working Design for Center Medallion.
The Japanese Letters are on page 19.

DIRECTIONS FOR FLAG—TABLE RUNNER

A hem 1/8 inch wide all around linen and crochet. Sc close together all around over hem.

2nd Row—Open meshes all around made by making a dc in every alternate sc of first row.

3rd Row—Sl st to center of open mesh * ch 3, sc in next sp, ch 3, sc in next sp. Ch 6 sc in same sp. Repeat from star all around.

CORNER

Ch 158, turn. **2nd Row**—50 open meshes, 1 bk, turn.

3rd Row—Sl st across bk. 1 bk. 49 open meshes, turn, follow design, making each row 1 bk shorter than the preceding one.

CENTER

Ch 149, turn. **2nd Row**—Solid blocks all across. Follow design till flag is finished. For design of letter, see alphabet on page 19.

WORKING DESIGNS FOR TABLE COVER

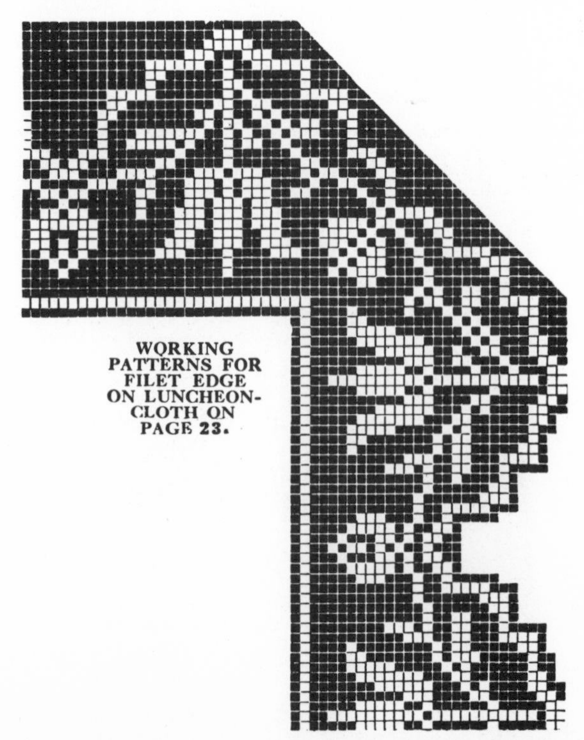

WORKING PATTERNS FOR FILET EDGE ON LUNCHEON-CLOTH ON PAGE 23.

Where Filet and Cross-Stitch Meet

DIRECTIONS FOR SQUARE CENTERPIECE.

Filet, crochet, cross-stitch in peasant embroidery and hand hemstitched.

MATERIALS—Coats Mercerized Crochet No. 100. No. 14 Hook.

MEDALLION.

Start at one edge, working crosswise.

Ch. 149.

1st Row—48 sp.

2nd Row—1 sp, 46 bl, 1 sp.

3rd Row, 4th, 5th and 6th rows—1 sp, 1 bl, 44sp, 1 bl, 1 sp.

7th Row—Start leaf and stem of design and continue to follow.

EDGE

Start at narrowest part, working crosswise.

Ch. 50.

1st Row—1 sp, 1 bl, 2 sp, 1 bl, 1 sp, 2 bl, 1 sp, 1 bl, 1 sp, 1 bl, 2 sp, 1 bl.

2nd Row—Add 1 bl at first side and continue to follow design, adding blocks at lower edge to form scallops. After one side and across corner if completed it will be necessary to break cotton and start on the side of corner and work the next side. Hem around edge and hem around medallion are hemstitched by hand.

CROSS-STITCH—Make on canvas 8 meshes to the inch with six strand floss, using the whole 6 strands, 1 skein each of Black, Dk. Moss Green 60, Dk. Yellow 43, China Blue 76, Lt. Red 6. Follow color chart on page 24.

WORKING PATTERNS FOR FILET AND CROSS-STITCH SHOWN ABOVE.

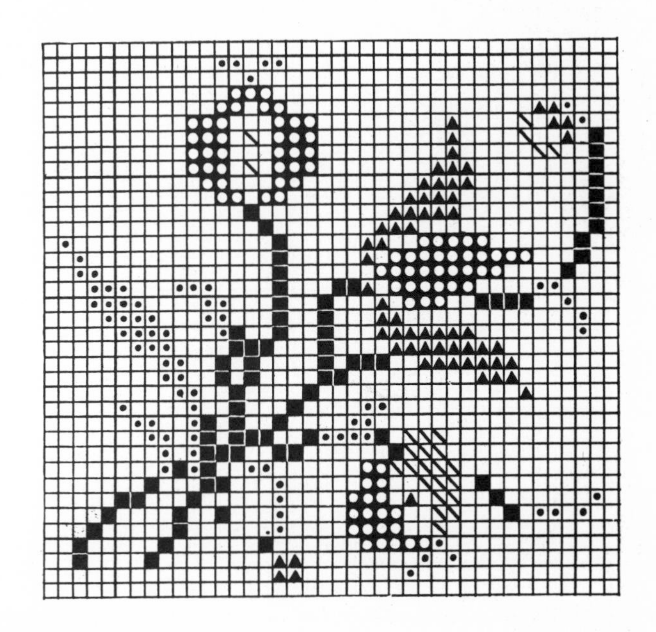

Springtime Centerpiece in Jonquils

DIRECTIONS FOR CROSS-STITCH

The rich colors of the Jonquil are selected for you by following the list of Coats Six Strand Floss mentioned below by the color chart, the working pattern of which is easy to follow. It is unusual in shape, which is made by placing the 8 filet medallions evenly spaced on a circle, and then drawing a line and making a point two inches deep between them, and having machine hemstitched, then following the crochet directions.

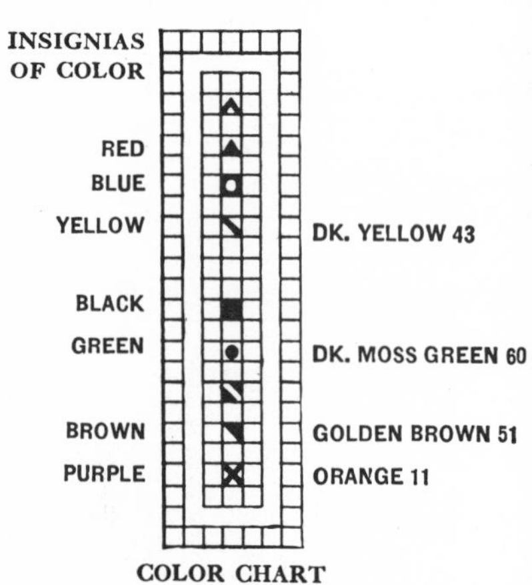

COLOR CHART

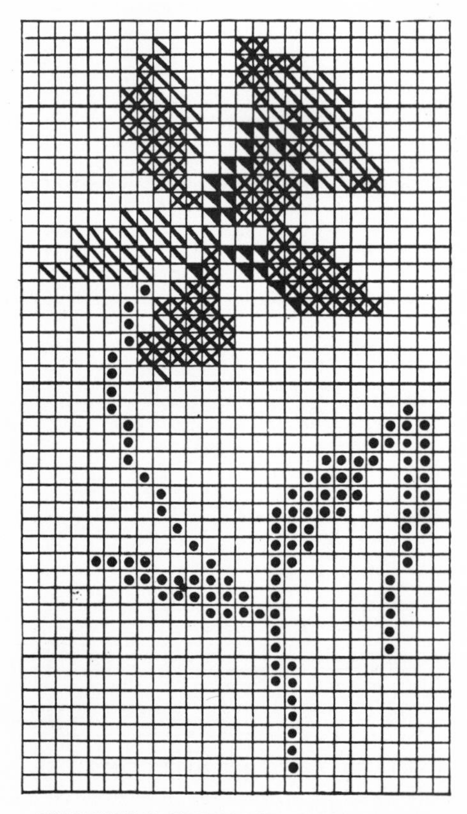

WORKING PATTERN FOR CROSS-STITCH

The charm of this piece is in the fact that both crochet and embroidery carry the same flower in design and also in the grace given it.

WORKING PATTERN FOR FILET.

DIRECTIONS FOR FILET IN CENTERPIECE.

MATERIALS—Coats Mercerized Crochet No. 60. No. 12 Hook.

INSET

Start at small end, working crosswise.

Ch 14.

1st Row—3 sp.

2nd 3rd and 4th Rows—1 sp, 1 bl, 1 sp.

5th Row—Add 1 sp at each end, and continue to add sp at each end, as shown in working plate, to form the shape. Make 8 insets and cut linen to fit them. Have it machine hemstitched. Cut linen 1/8 inch outside of hemstitching, crochet all around, 1 s st in each hole of hemstitching, sew in the insets, crochet edge all around, as follows: 1 s st in s st, ch 3, 1 s st in 2nd s st, * 1 p, ch 3, 1 s st in 2nd s st, ch 3, 1 s st in 2nd s st, repeat from *.

Sweater Scarf

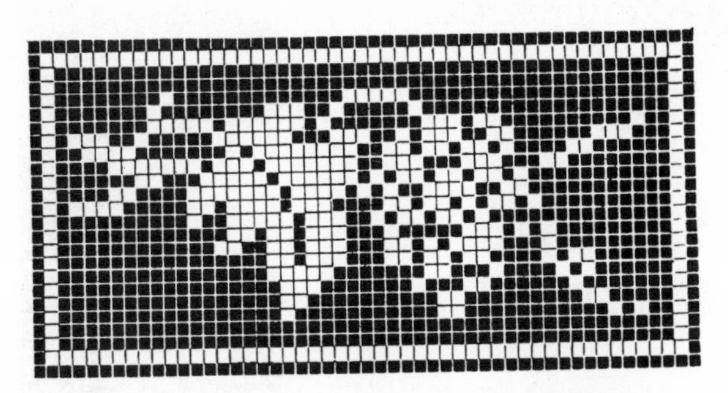

WORKING DESIGN FOR SCARF BORDER

DETAIL OF STITCH IN SCARF

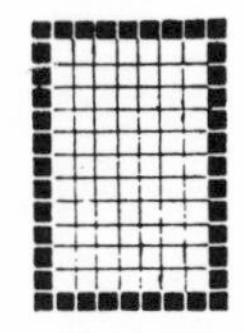

WORKING PATTERN FOR BELT

DIRECTIONS FOR SWEATER SCARF

SCARF

MATERIALS—Coats Pearl Cotton, No. 5. No. 2 Hook. Lavender for an old lady, or pink or blue for the young girl, making the border 3 meshes to the inch.

Commence at one end, working cross-wise.

Ch. 150.

1st Row—49 bl.

2nd and 3rd Rows—Each 1 bl, 47 sp, 1 bl.

4th Row—Follow design.

Make the other end of scarf like first one.

CENTER

Join the two ends with a ch of 312, on which make the following:

1st Row—8 tr in 4th st of ch, skip 3 st of ch, 1 s st in next st, repeat to end of ch. Break cotton.

2nd Row—Start at beginning of 1st row, fasten cotton, ch 4, fasten with sl st between 2nd and 3rd bl of filet end, ch 4 * throw cotton over, draw up a loop in 1st tr below, always taking up back loop only, throw cotton over, draw through 2 sts only, retaining the remaining loops on hook, repeat from * 3 times, there will now be 5 loops on the hook, throw cotton over and draw through all 5 loops, ch 4, 1 s st in 4 tr below, ch 4, * take up one in each of the 4 remaining tr of 1st shell, 1 in s st and 1 in each of the 1st 4 tr of 2nd shell below, you will have 10 loops on the hook, throw cotton over and draw through the 10 loops, ch 4, 1 s st in top of shell of last row, ch 4, repeat from last *, join last end with sl st to the other filet end between 2nd and 3rd bl. Break cotton.

3rd Row—Fasten cotton in filet end 1 bl from where 2nd row was joined to end. 4 tr in center of inverted shell of 2nd row, * 1 s st in 1 st of last row, 8 tr in next inverted shell of 2nd row, repeat from *.

Fasten last end to other filet end 1 bl from where 2nd row was fastened.

4th Row—Fasten cotton in filet end in the same place as 3rd row, ch 4, * take up one in each of the 4 tr of last row, 1 in s st and 1 in each of the 1st 4 tr of 2nd shell below, you will have 10 loops on the hook, throw cotton over and draw through the 10 loops, ch 4, 1 s st in top of shell of last row, ch 4, repeat from *, join in same st as last row at filet end. Break cotton.

5th Row—Fasten cotton in same st as last row, * 8 tr in center of inverted sh, 1 s st in s st of last row, repeat from *, join at same place on the other end.

Repeat the 2nd, 3rd, 4th, and 5th rows, when joining allow a row of filet to a row of shell.

FRINGE ACROSS ENDS

Cut the cotton in pieces, 15 inches long, loop 4 pieces in each bl across each end, take half of first group and half of second group and tie together in a hard knot. Continue across.

BELT

Ch. 24.

1st Row—7 bl.

Repeat row until belt is the required length.

COVER FOR BUTTON MOLD

Ch 3, join in ring.

1st Row—2 s st in each st of ch.

2nd Row—2 s st in each st, taking up back loop only.

3rd Row—* 1 s st in 1st 2 st, 2 s st in next st, repeat from *.

Repeat 3rd row until there are 6 rows in all and till cover measures 2 inches in diameter.

SMALL TASSELS AT BUTTONS

Cut cotton in pieces 12 inches long, fold pieces in center; take 8 pieces for each tassel; loop pieces of cotton through the double end of tassel, fasten the cotton under button, take another piece of cotton and wind 3 times around tassel about half inch from top; tie tight

Rose Yoke with Sleeves

MATERIALS—Five balls Coats Six Cord Mercerized Crochet Cotton No. 50.

Ch 84, turn, allowing 8 for turning, then make 22 more sps and 4 dc. Continue across front and when last filet is made make 9 rows of sps at lower end of yoke, at every other row leaving 2 sps off. This will form the under part of sleeve. Break thread and start up at neck with 23 sps and continue around to back, then turn in same with 23 sps, making 4 dc at neck and 1 sp each time. Continue across for back same as front, then turn again with same number of sps to make the other shoulder piece and at both back and front make the 9 rows of meshes which is to form under part of sleeve. Break thread and start sleeve by making 10 blocks and continue around with sps, fastening in top of shoulder sps, continuing around with same design as on front, only making one rose in center top of sleeve and leaves on either side.

For edging and beading fill in each sp with dc.

Row 2—Ch 2 and dc in every 3d dc. Continue around.

Row 3—Triple treble in each dc, with 2 ch between tr tr.

Row 4—Dc in each tr tr, with 2 ch between dc.

Row 5—In one sp work 5 tr tr, with 2 ch between, 1 sc in next sp, repeat around.

Row 6—Ch 3 and fasten in top of each triple tr, repeat.

Scallop Yoke

MATERIALS—Two balls Coats Six Cord Mercerized Crochet Cotton No. 50.

Ch 12, join.

Row 1—32 dc.

Row 2—32 sc.

Row 3—4 sc, 4 ch, * 1 h tr of 3 stitches, 4 ch, repeat around from *.

Row 4—4 sc on 4 sc, 2 sc on 4 ch; 4 ch, * 2 dc, 3 ch, 2 dc in each loop of 4 ch with 2 dc between, repeat around from *.

Row 5—2 sc over 4 ch, sc over sc with 2 on 4 ch, 4 ch, * in each loop of 3 ch, work a shell of 3 dc, 3 ch, 3 dc, 3 ch, repeat around.

Row 6—Same as Row 5 except 4 ch between. From now on, in each row work sc over sc, 2 sc over ch at each side of sc and a ch of 4 between the shells and the sc.

Row 7—Shell in shell, ch 4, fasten over center of 2 previous loops, 4 ch, repeat.

Row 8—Ch 12, fasten in top of shell. Repeat around.

Row 9—20 dc over each 12 ch.

Row 10—5 h tr of 4 st each with 4 ch between, over each 20 dc.

Row 11—2 sc, 1 p, 2 sc in each loop.

When desired number of medallions are made, join and make 3 or 4 rows of knot-stitch. Then ch 5 and fasten in each knot-stitch, which will make yoke round. Next put 1 h tr of 4 st each over each 5 ch with 4 ch between. Last row, same as edge of medallion.

Deep Yoke of Butterflies

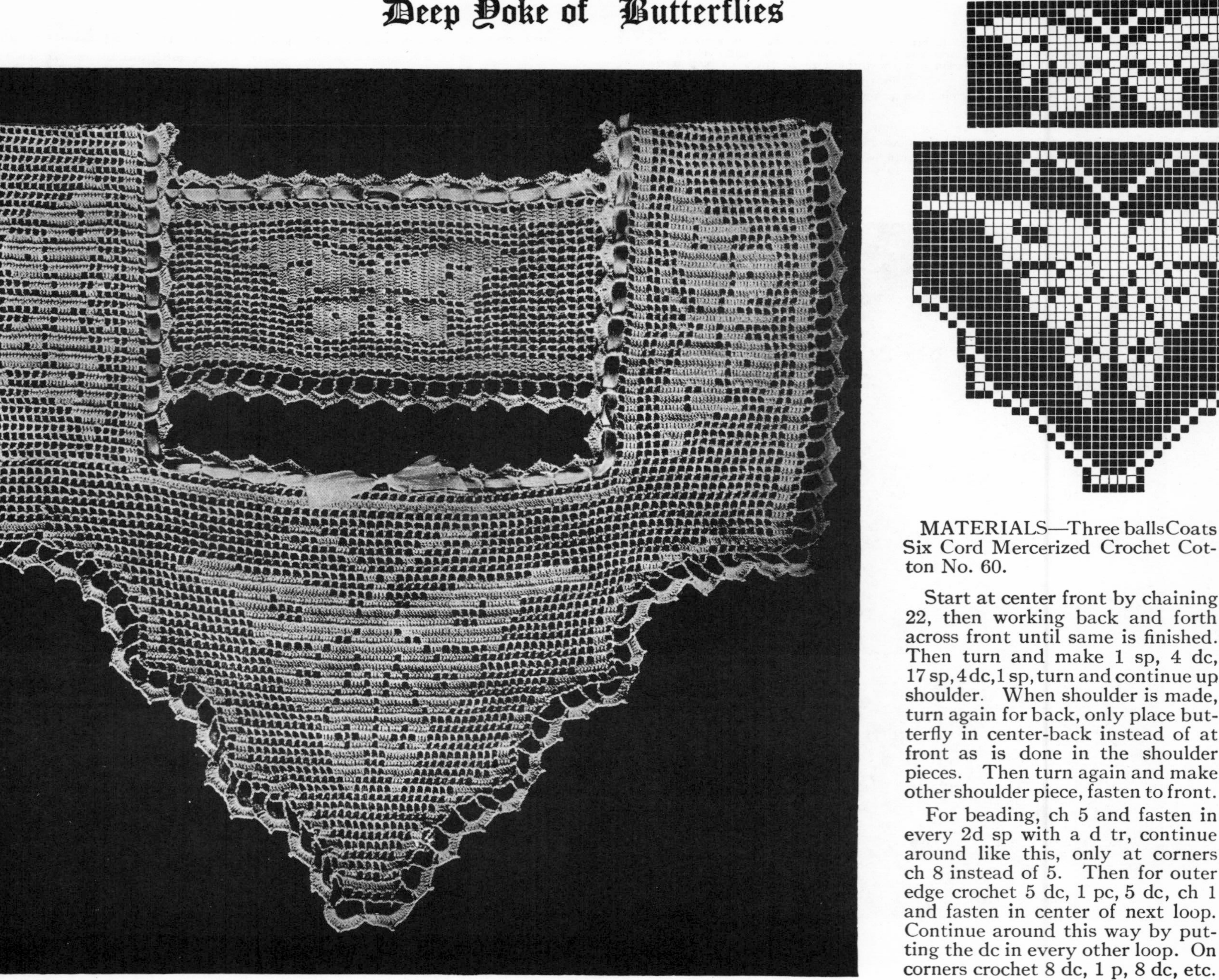

MATERIALS—Three balls Coats Six Cord Mercerized Crochet Cotton No. 60.

Start at center front by chaining 22, then working back and forth across front until same is finished. Then turn and make 1 sp, 4 dc, 17 sp, 4 dc, 1 sp, turn and continue up shoulder. When shoulder is made, turn again for back, only place butterfly in center-back instead of at front as is done in the shoulder pieces. Then turn again and make other shoulder piece, fasten to front.

For beading, ch 5 and fasten in every 2d sp with a d tr, continue around like this, only at corners ch 8 instead of 5. Then for outer edge crochet 5 dc, 1 pc, 5 dc, ch 1 and fasten in center of next loop. Continue around this way by putting the dc in every other loop. On corners crochet 8 dc, 1 p, 8 dc, etc.

Gown Yoke with Sleeves

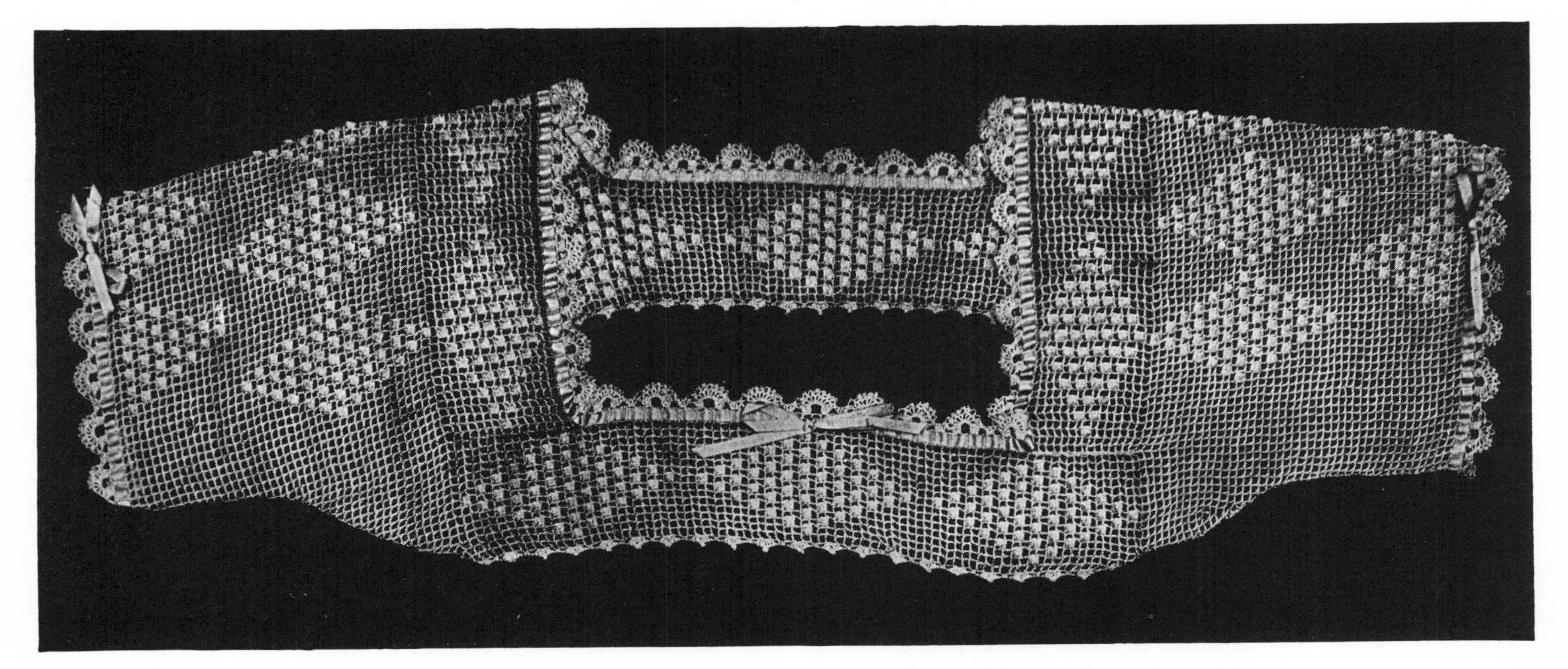

MATERIALS—Three balls Coats Six Cord Mercerized Crochet Cotton No. 20.

For the sleeve make a ch of 258 sts.

Rows 1–2—84 meshes.

Row 3—31 m, * 1 pc st (pop-corn), 1 m, repeat from * until you have 7 pc, 3 m, repeat 7 pc st, with m between, 31 m.

Row 4—Plain.

Row 5—32 m, 6 pc, m between each, 5 m, 1 pc, 1 m, till you have 6 pc, 32 m.

Row 6—Plain.

Row 7—5 pc, each row of pc diminishes until you have 1 pc, 13 m, 1 pc, with 37 m at beginning and end. Then 2 plain rows.

Row 18—30 m, 1 pc, 13 m, 1 pc, 13 m, 1 pc, 30 m.

Row 19—Plain.

From now you increase number of pc each time until you have 7, then decrease to 1 again. Beginning with the 24th row, add one sp at the end of each row, until you have added 8 sps on each side. When you have completed the 3 diamond-shaped groups the sleeve has 1 plain row which finishes it. For the strip over the shoulder make a strip 15 m wide with 2 diamond-shaped groups of pc, and for front and back same width strip with 3 diamond-shaped groups; join together and finish neck and sleeves like the picture.

Shamrock Yoke

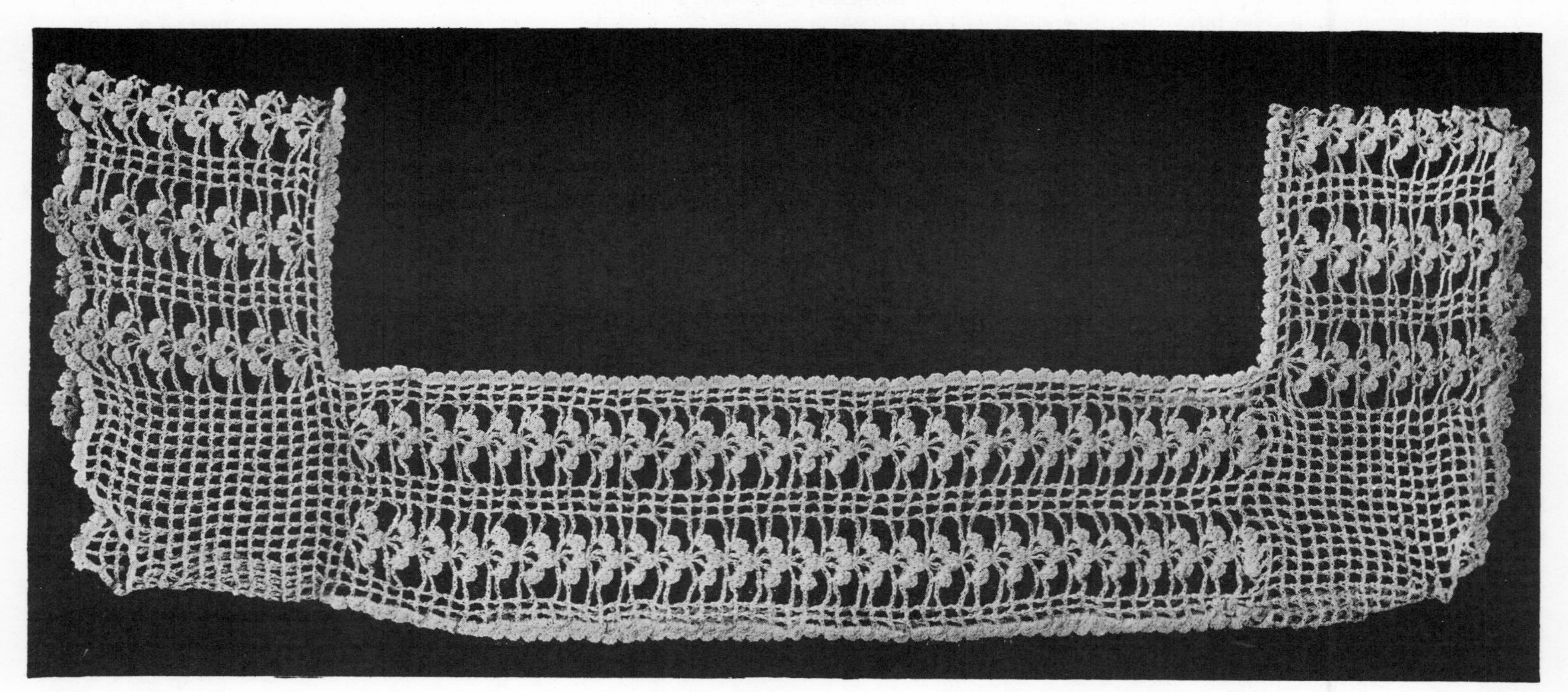

MATERIALS—Two balls Coats Mercerized Crochet Cotton No. 50.

Ch 55, turn.

Row 1—16 sp, ch 5, turn.

Row 2—*Make 2 sp, ch 3, skip 2 sp, a shell of 4 trs (thread over twice), with 2 ch between trs in next sp, ch 3, skip 2 sp, * repeat from first star, 2 sp, ch 5, turn.

Row 3—2 sps, ch 3, * sc into top of first tr of shell, fill ch of sh with 5 dc, repeat twice, ch 3, 2 sp, * repeat all between two stars, ch 5, turn.

Begin again at 2d row, and repeat until you have a strip long enough to go across the front. Make a strip the same for the back. In this yoke there are 27 rows of shamrocks.

Make shoulders in same manner, working 7 rows of 6 shamrocks each, on each shoulder. The space under the arm is of plain spaces. In making a ch, allow 3 sts for every space, plus 1 for the outside bar; whenever you turn ch 5, for one side and the top of 1st sp of next row. The finish at the edges of this yoke is like the leaves of the shamrock.

Directions for Medallion Yoke

MATERIALS—For Butterfly, one ball No. 20; and for Medallions, two balls No. 80; all of Coats Six Cord Mercerized Crochet Cotton.

There are 10 Medallions, 11 wheels each. Place butterfly in front, and fasten all together with needle and thread.

For wheel, ch 8, join. In this ring make * 4 groups of 4 dc, with p between groups. Ch 12, join last 8 of these in a ring, leaving 4 of the ch for a link between wheels. Repeat from star until you have 7 half wheels with 4 ch between. For the 8th wheel, you fill the ring with 8 groups, with 7 p; join into middle of ch of 4. Fill the other side of wheels in same way back to 1st. In this wheel make two groups of 4 dc, and at the 2nd p * ch 16, sl st into central p of next wheel, ch 8, sl st into center of 16 ch, ch 8, sl st into p of next wheel, * repeat until the 8 wheels have 8 spokes of double chains. Then fill in the 8th group of dc, and join. Make three more wheels, as you made the 8 in joining the wheel at the lower point of the Medallion, leave 5 p for the bottom, and only one between the joining of the other wheels.

BUTTERFLY—Ch 4, sk 1, 3 sc, turn. 4 sc (2 sc into first, 2 sc into next 2 sts), turn. 5 sc, turn. 6 sc, turn. 2 more rows of 6 sc, turn. 1 row of 5 sc, turn. 4 sc, turn, 3 sc, turn. 2 sc, turn. 3 sc, turn. 4 sc, turn. 5 sc, turn. 6 sc, turn. 7 sc, turn. 8 sc, turn. 9 sc, turn. 10 sc, turn. 11 sc, turn. 4 more rows of 11 sc, turn. Decrease one st in each row until 2 sc are left, turn. Increase one st in each row until 9 sc. 2 more rows 9 sc, turn. Decrease until 1 sc. Work around body to center of head, * 1 sc into each st. Ch 17, sk 1, * cotton over hook, insert into st and repeat from * three times more, then pull through all loops. 25 sc around the chain of ch 17, this makes 1 feeler, repeat, and 1 sc into each st around other side of body.

DAISY—Ch 8, join, 12 sc into ring, join, * into first st, 1 sc, 1 h dc, 1 dc, 1 tc, 1 dtc, ch 5, form p, 1 dtc, 1 dc, 1 h dc, 1 sc, sk 1, and repeat from * 5 times. Make 1 more daisy for other wing.

RINGS—Ch 4, join with sl st. Ch 5, 1 dc, ch 2, 1 dc, in ring, repeat with 1 dc, 2 ch until there are 6 dc, ch 2, join. 6 sc over ch 2, p, repeat around, join. Make 3 more rings.

SMALL WING—Sc at curve between body and tail, 1 sc ch 5, 1 sc into p of ring, ch 5, 1 sc into next p, ch 6, 1 dc into next p, ch 6, 1 dc into same, ch 6, 1 sc into following p, ch 5, 1 sc into next p, ch 10, 1 sc into next p, ch 5, 1 sc into same st of body where the wing commenced, turn. 8 sc around last ch 5, 8 sc around ch 10, ch 5, sk 8 sts of body, 1 sc, ch 5, 1 sc into center between 2 bars, 8 sc around ch 5, 1 sl st into body, 7 sc into each hole around ring, 2 sc into sts of body, turn, 7 sc, 1 p, 5 sc, 1 p, 5 sc, 1 p, 5 sc, 1 p, 3 sc, 1 p, 3 sc, 1 p, 5 sc, 1 p, 5 sc, 1 p, 19 sc, 1 sc into body, finish off.

LARGE WING—Start at left side of body between head and body, ch 7, sk 3, 1 sc, ch 7, sk 4, 1 sc, ch 4, 1 sc into 4th st of small wing, turn, 6 sc around ch 4, 4 sc around other ch, join into p of ring, 4 sc around same ch, 4 sc around next ch, join to next p of ring, ch 8, 1 sc into next p, turn, 5 sc around ch 8, turn, ch 10, 1 sc into same p, ch 4, 1 sc into next p, join to point of daisy petal, ch 6, 1 sc into next point of petal, turn, 8 sc into loop, 5 sc into next loop, 8 sc into following loop, turn, ch 5, 1 sc into same point, ch 6, 1 sc into next point, ch 10, 1 sc into following point, turn. 6 sc around ch, turn. Ch 10, 1 sc into same p, turn. 6 sc around ch, turn. Ch 6, 1 sc into next point, ch 6, 1 sc into following point, ch 7, 1 sc into joining between daisy and ring, ch 4, 1 sc into next p, ch 12, turn. 1 sc into the outside point of daisy, 8 sc around ch leading to joining of daisy and ring, 1 sl st into sp, 6 sc around ch, 1 sl st into next sp, 8 sc around next ch, turn. Ch 0, 1 sc into same p, turn. 6 sc around ch, ch 3, 1 sc into 7tn st of small wing, ch 3, 1 sc into next p of ring, ch 3, 1 sc in beginning of large wing, turn, 4 sc around ch 3, 4 sc around next ch 3, 4 sc around next ch 3, join to p of small wing, 8 sc into each loop around big wing. Into last 2 loops, 5 sc, 2 sl st into body, turn, 1 sc into each st around wing at end, 1 sc into same p, turn. 5 sc, 1 p, 5 sc, repeat around. At end join with sl st to body. Make 2 more wings for other side of body.

Butterfly Yoke

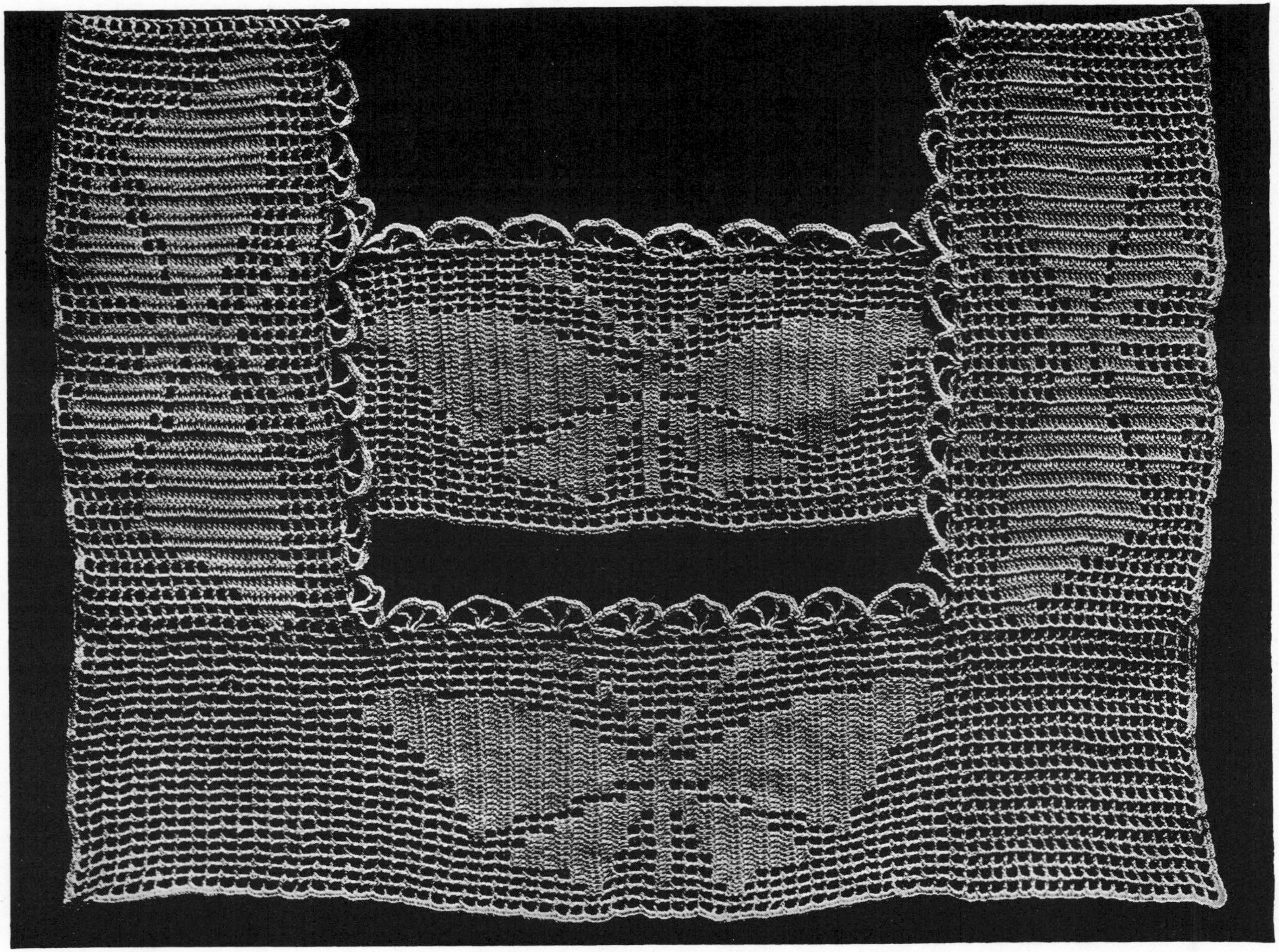

MATERIALS—Two balls Coats Six Cord Mercerized Crochet Cotton No. 60.

Ch 68, turn and make 19 rows of 21 sps each, then start butterfly. For back and front pieces have 21 sps and for shoulder pieces just have 19 sps for width of lace.

Outer edge is 4 sc in each sp.

Inner edge is made by putting 4 tr tr in every 5th sp, skipping 4 sps between, then sc over middle stitch between shells.

Irish Crochet Yoke

DIRECTIONS FOR IRISH CROCHET YOKE

MATERIALS—Coats Mercerized Crochet No. 50. Hook No. 12.

For the Small Rose

Ch 5, join.

1st Row—In each st make 1 tr, ch 2, repeat around.

This makes 5 spaces.

2nd Row—In each space make 1 s st, 4 trs 1 s st.

3rd Row—Ch 3, fasten at the bottom of the first leaf at the back. Ch. 4, fasten in same place on 2nd leaf. Repeat this ch of 4 for each leaf.

4th Row—Over these chains make the second row of leaves, adding 1 tr (1sst, 5 trs, 1 s st).

For the Large Roses

Make six spaces and three rows of leaves. Adding trs as the leaves grow larger.

These roses have the leaves over the intersections.

The large roses have loops of 3 ch around each row of leaves.

To Make Leaves—

Ch. 11.

Turn, s st into 4th ch from the needle. *Make s st in each st to bottom ch 3. Turn and go up the other side. Never go clear to the top. Always leave two sts. Turn and ch 3. Go down to the bottom, making 6 s st on the leaf, the 7th in the loop at the bottom turn, ch 3, make a st in the loop and 5 more up the leaf. In making these ribbed leaves you always use the back half of the st.

The leaves are attached to the last leaf you make. Make a ch as long as you wish your stem. Ten sts below the top leaf fasten a pair of leaves and ten sts below that fasten another pair. Then make 3 s sts the length of the stem.

The Lilies of the Valley are made like the leaves, only very small. Each one.has a stem of 5 ch. The top one has a ch long enough for the whole stem. The bells are attached about 10 or 12 ch apart, all hanging one way. Cover the whole stem with s st.

For the Center Medallion

Ch 9, join.

1st Row—2 s st in each st.

2nd Row—* 1 tr, 3 ch, * repeat around until you have 9 spaces. Pick up the cord, fasten in very firmly 4 thicknesses, cover this closely with 2 s st, turn and work another row back, picking up back of st only. Fasten the cord firmly and cut off If necessary to keep the work flat add a st once in a while. For the next row ch 6, skip 4, s st in next, repeat around. Cover these loops with s st and picots. Put three leaves on each side and fasten firmly.

Baste motifs firmly into place on a piece of black oilcloth. Make a ch long enough for the bottom of the yoke and another for the top. Fill the chs with s st. Baste firmly into place and fill as follows: ch 4, 1 p, ch 4.

To make an open row for the ribbon make a ch long enough to go around the yoke, fill with s st, *ch 10 for the first bar, fasten to the yoke. 3 s st in the yoke, ch 5, fasten with short tr in the middle of the 1st bar, ch 5, fasten to the top ch, 3 sts from where the 1st bar started. 8 s st in next 8 sts of top ch. Ch 10, join to yoke, 8 sts beyond 1st two bars. 8 s st in yoke and repeat from *.

For the next row ch 7, skip 4 sts, s st in each of next 2 sts, repeat around 2nd row of edge which is the last. *3 s st over the first loop, p, 9 s st to finish loop, s st between loops, 6 s st in next loop, ch 7, turn and fasten in 6th st of 1st scallop. Turn again and fill this top loop with 3 s st, p, 3 s st, p, 3 s st, p, 3 s st, p, then on the last half of the second scallop 3 s st, p, 3 s st, fasten down between scallops. This finishes one point of these scallops. Repeat from * all around.

Violet Corset Cover in Filet

DIRECTIONS

MATERIALS—J. & P. Coats Mercerized Crochet Cotton, No. 40. Milward's Steel Crochet Needle, No. 13.

At center of front, where garment opens, add the number of open meshes to make the desired bust measure, this measuring for 32 bust.

Ch 207, and make 4 rows of 67 sp each. For the front, follow plate No. 78, for 46 rows, when the decrease begins, as shown. Work 17 rows all spaces, then begin working at the bottom edge of chart (p. 35) increasing as shown until there are 61 sp. Then ch 180 and work 58 additional sp for the shoulder strap, which is 17 rows wide, with the pattern worked as shown. Drop 58 sp and work the back from Plate No. 81. Make the other shoulder strap and front like the first, dropping off or adding on for armhole, as on the other side.

FOR THE WAIST—Work 2 s st in 1st sp, 1 s st in 2d sp, repeat across and turn. **2d Row**—Tr in each st, turn.

FOR BROAD BELT—Ch 32, turn. On this ch work 9 sp, sl st to bottom of waist, turn. 9 sp, turn. 9 sp back, sl st to waist, turn. Ch 32 for the strip with the violet, follow design for 11 rows. Then ch 32 and work 3 rows of sp, as at first. Continue alternating the violets with the spaces. Make a row of sp across the bottom, then a row of tr. Finish with a row of s st across bottom and up both fronts. Around neck and arm edges, make a row of d tr spaces, for ribbon, on this a row of regular sp, and finish edge with a row of shells of 8 d tr, with p between, skip 2 sp, s st in next, shell in next 3d sp, and repeat.

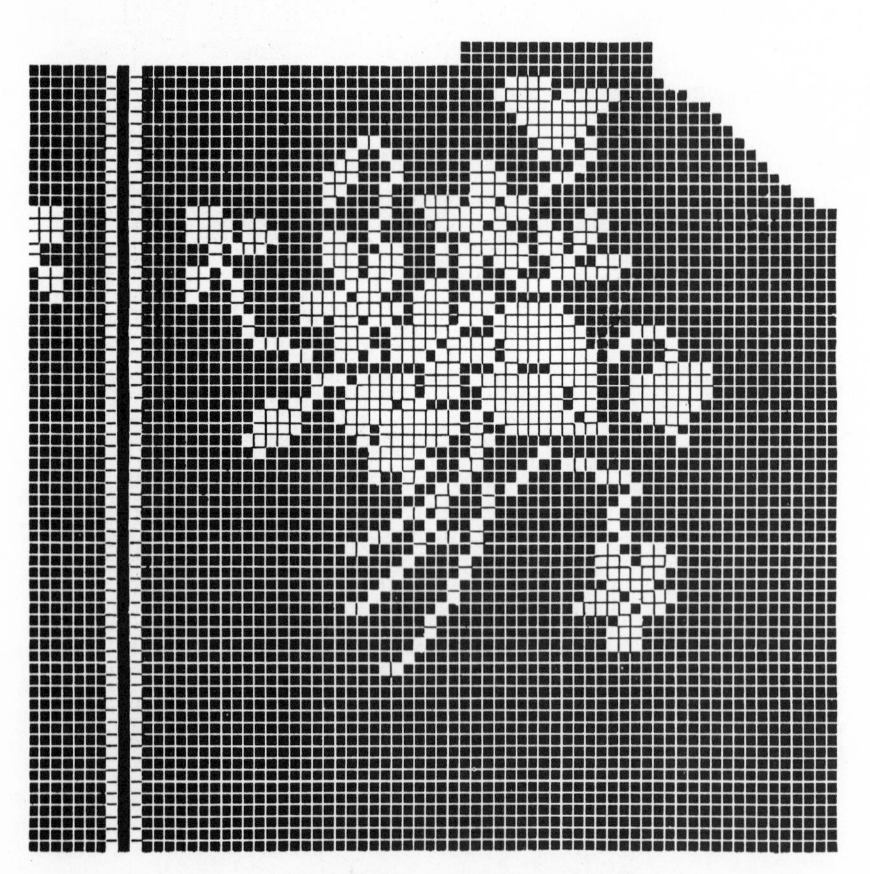

Working design for front of Corset Cover.

Chart is for front of corset cover and joins back under arm just as chart for back is cut.

Working Designs for Back, Shoulder Straps and Belt for the Violet Corset Cover

BACK AND SHOULDERS

Long Sweater with Long Sleeves

Directions for this sweater appear on page 38.

Working Pattern for Long Sweater with Long Sleeves

Directions for this sweater appear on page 38.

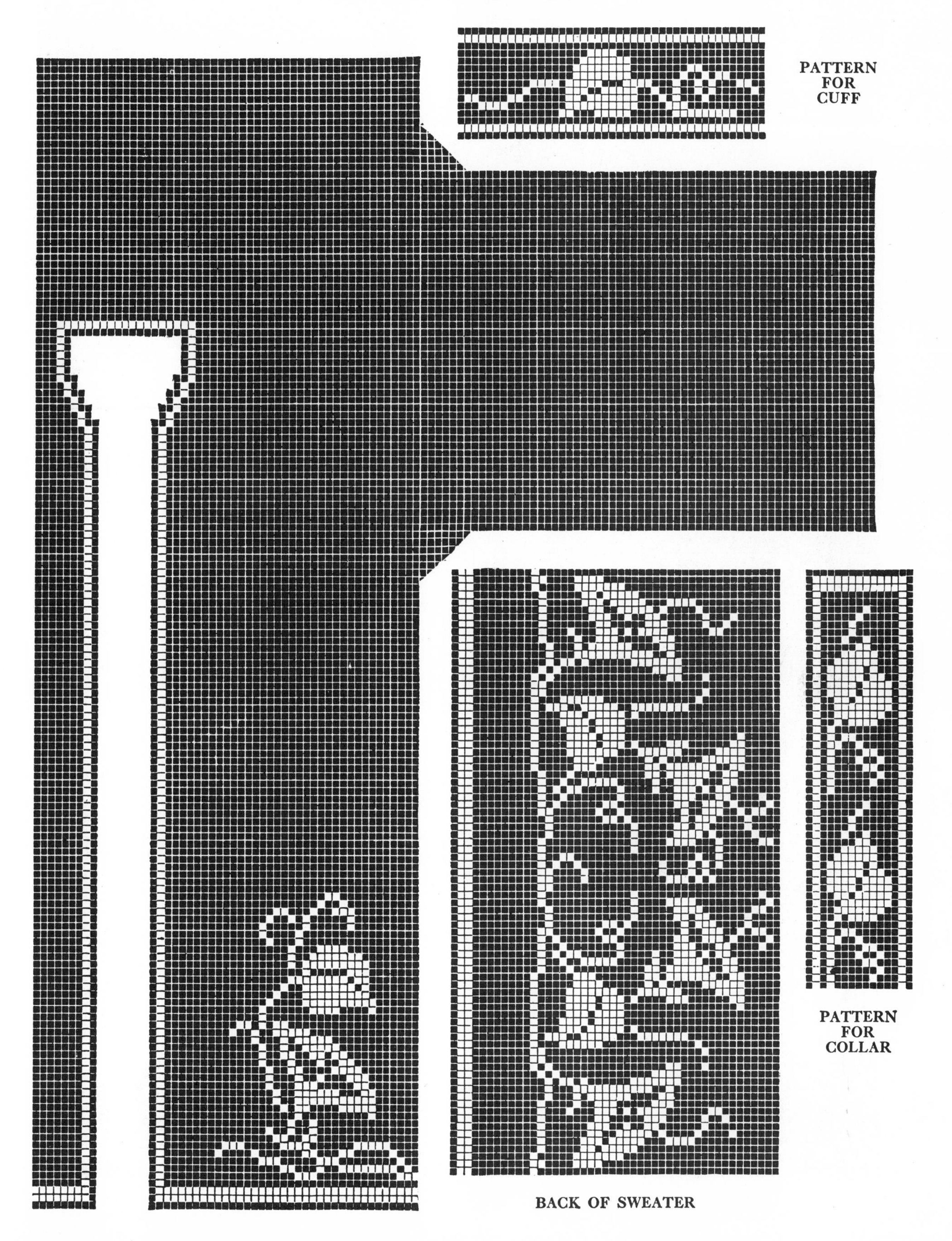

Long Sweater with Long Sleeves

See pages 36 and 37.

DIRECTIONS

MATERIALS—Coats "Silk Finish" Crochet Cotton. No. 2 Hook. 4 meshes to the inch.

Start at lower end of back, working cross-wise.

Ch. 246.

1st and 2nd Rows—Each, 81 bl.

Next 8 Rows—Each, 81 sp.

Next Row—Starting Morning Glory design and follow.

After 89 rows are completed add 1 sp at each end of each row for 7 rows.

Next row add 54 sp at each end for sleeves, after the 54 sp have been added continue to work across the entire width till 20 rows have been completed, then leave off the 17 center meshes for back of neck and allthe meshes on one side of it, working on the meshes on the side for one sleeve and one front. When the sleeve is 45 meshes wide drop off 54 meshes for the sleeve, and on the next 7 rows leave off one mesh on each row for under arm. Continue to work down the front until it is as long under arm as the back was making the Morning G.ory as shown in design.

Break cotton and start back at shoulder. Make 2nd sleeve and front like the first one. Sew up sleeves and under arm.

Band For Cuff—

Start at one end and work up and down.

Ch. 38.

1st and 2nd Rows—11 sp.

3rd Row—Start Morning Glory and follow design, sew up and sew to lower edge of sleeve.

Band up front and around neck the same width as cuff, following design.

Edge around cuff and band 1 row solid blocks with a p between every 3rd and 9th bl.

Sash—

Start at one end, working cross-wise.

Ch 27.

1st Row—8 bl.

Repeat 1st row till sash is 2¼ yards long. Finish ends with fringe.

Keepers for Sash—

Ch. 33.

1st Row—10 bl.

Sew one keeper to each under arm seam.

Baby Collar

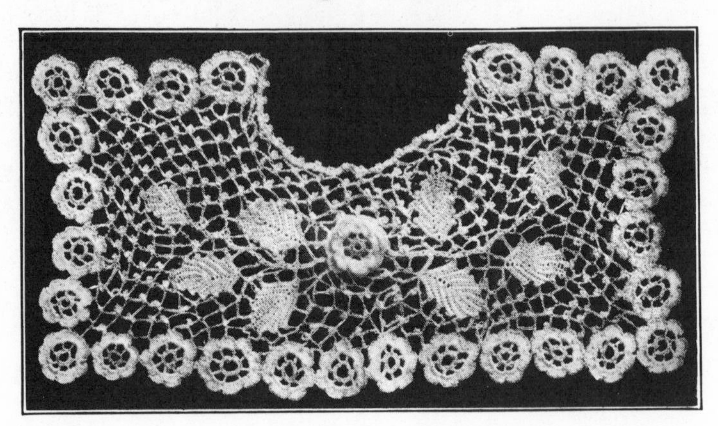

DIRECTIONS

MATERIALS—J. & P. Coats Mercerized Crochet Cotton, No. 100.

The rose in the center is made by the directions for Irish Crochet Collar, on page 39, using only two rows of petals, and allowing for seven petals in each row.

For small leaf, ch 11, 1 s st into 4th from needle, 1 s st in each of next 7, 3 s st into end chain and 8 s st up the other side of chain, ch 3, turn. Repeat for the required number of ribs, having 8 s st each side of the central sts, always putting the needle in the back of the stitch. The large leaves are started with a chain of thirteen and have ten stitches each side of the central three; they have seventeen ribs.

The row of single roses is made as are the other roses, working only one row of petals. For making the yoke, follow the method used in shaping the Irish collar on page 39.

Irish Crochet Collar and Cuffs

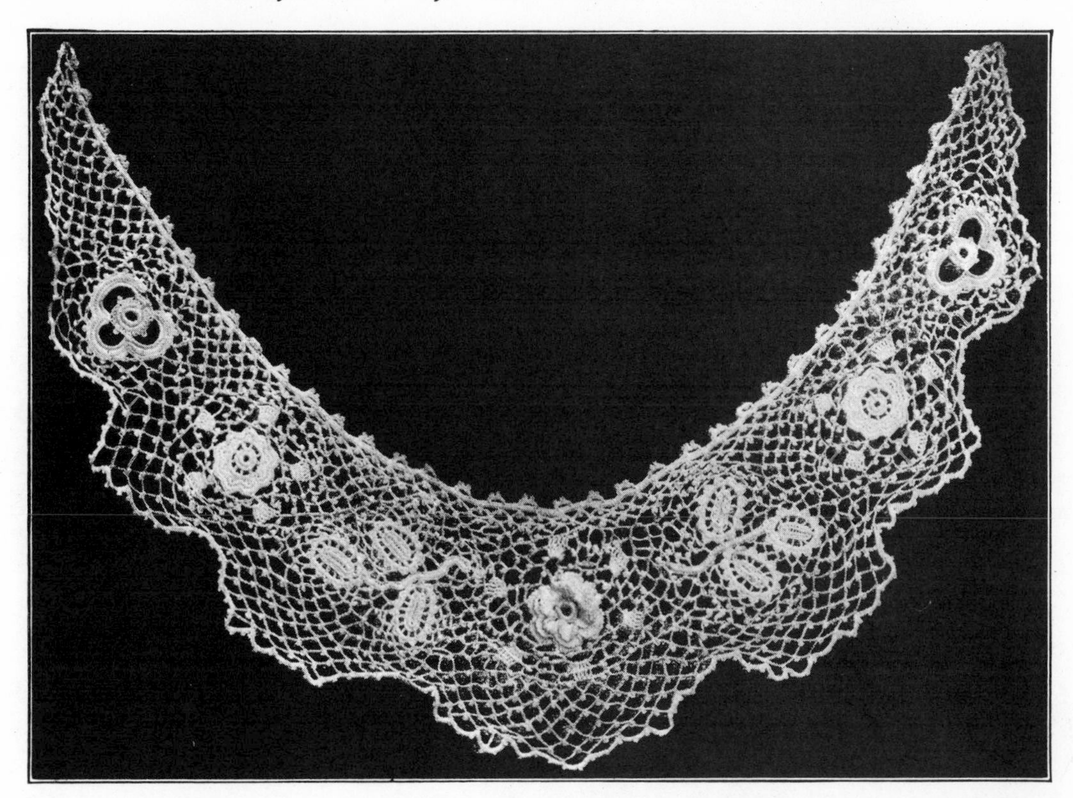

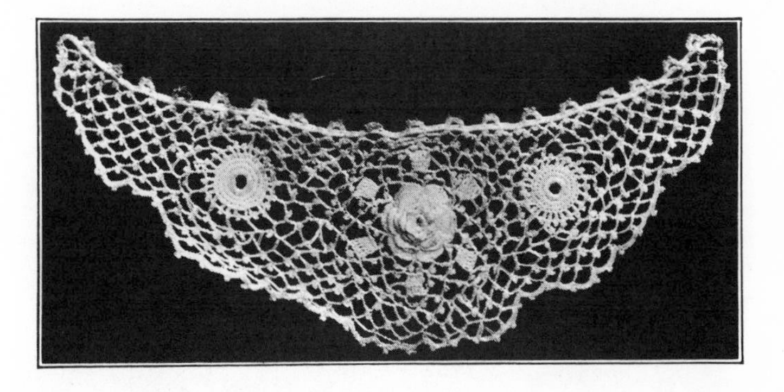

DIRECTIONS

MATERIALS—J. & P. Coats Mercerized Crochet Cotton, No. 70. 1 ball padding cotton.

First make the motifs; 1 double rose for collar, one for each cuff. Six leaves for collar, 2 single roses for collar, two for each cuff, and two shamrocks for collar.

FOR THE ROSE IN CENTER—Wind padding cotton twice around a small pencil, cover this ring with 18 sc. **1st Row**—*1 tr, 1 ch, six times, join. In each of these sp, 1 tr, 4 d tr, 1 tr, join. **2d Row**—Back of each leaf ch 3, fastening between with 1 s st. **3d Row**—In these ch make another row of leaves each 1 tr, 7 d tr, 1 tr, join. **4th Row**—Six times, 4 ch. **5th Row**—6 leaves, each 1 tr, 10 d tr, 1 tr, sl st. **6th Row**—In edge of outside row of leaves ch 3, sl st, repeat. **7th Row**—Make 12 loops around the rose, of 3 ch, p, 3 ch, each. **8th Row**—13 loops. **9th Row**—5 tr in 1st loop, ch 3, p, ch 3, tr, in next loop, ch 3, p, ch 3, tr in same loop, ch 3, p, ch 3, tr in next loop, repeat five times. You will then have 6 groups of 5 tr, 3 loops between groups. **Next Row**—Tr in tr with four loops between groups.

FOR THE STEM OF THE LEAVES—Ch 40. Take up the padding cord, double the end, s st in the loop, s st over both threads, taking one st of ch each time, to make the cord secure, cut off the short end close, 20 s st over this cord and the ch, leave the end of the cord that is fastened, for the end of stem, cut off about 4 inches for the rest of stem. Fasten another piece of the cord to the stem at the end of the 20 sts, work 15 s st over the cord. Turn, over the cord and into the back of the 10th st, work 10 s st. Drop the cord, 5 ch, 1 tr into end of leaf close to stem, around the leaf make a row of 15 sp, pick up cord, over it work into each sp, 1 s st, 4 tr, 1 s st, fasten to stem. On the other side of it make another leaf. Keep cord smooth and work flat; pick up the 4 inch cord and cover it with 20 s st and make your third leaf.

FOR THE SINGLE FLOWER—Make ring as you did for rose, make 9 sp around it, over the cord work in each sp 1 s st, 1 tr, 3 d tr, 1 tr, 1 s st. In the edge of each of these petals, over cord, make 12 st. Cut off cord and fasten securely.

FOR SHAMROCK—Make ring, over the cord, into this 32 s st. Drop cord, s st into every st, between 4th and 5th make p, (8 p). * ch 30, sl st into 2d p, repeat twice, turn; over cord, into each st of the 30 ch, a s st, picking up back part of st only, turn; over cord all around the three loops 3 s st, p, 3 s st. Be sure to draw the cord in such a way as to keep work smooth and in shamrock form. Cut off cord and fasten end securely.

Cut a pattern of shape desired, and baste the motifs firmly into position. Ch a piece long enough to go all around collar and baste that firmly around the edge. This pattern should be much larger than the collar, and this strip of ch should be strongly basted where the edge of collar should be. Fill between motifs and collar edge with crackle st, that is, chains and picots in rows, not necessarily regular. Around the edge, cover the ch with s st and p.

FOR THE CUFF—The double rose has five rows of petals, commencing like the rose for collar. The single rose has three rows of s st worked over the cord, then a row of spaces, with p between trs. Then a row of 3 ch, p, 3 ch, fastened in every 2d sp. Finish by directions for collar.

Pointed Yoke

ROSE YOKE OR COLLAR IN TABS

DIRECTIONS FOR POINTED YOKE

MATERIALS—Coats Mercerized Crochet, No. 70. Hook No. **14**.

Start at lower edge of point on left sleeve, working cross-wise.

Ch 5.

1st Row—1 bl.

2nd Row—Add 1 bl at each edge, 1 bl, 1 sp, 1 bl.

Continue to add bl at each edge as shown in design until the point on shoulder is wide enough, then add meshes for the front and back, after it is made up to the side of neck leave off the front and work around the back, after that is finished break cotton and start back at shoulder and make the front, after that is finished join the back and front on right shoulder and work down the right sleeve.

BEADING AND EDGE AROUND NECK

1st Row—Start at top of block, chain six, two d t r in second block, chain 4 repeat from star.

2nd Row—Start and chain 4, * chain 6, one treble in 2nd chain of 4, one p, one more treble in same place, chain 6, one sl st in 2 nd ch 4, repeat from *.

DIRECTIONS FOR COLLAR OR YOKE IN TABS

MATERIALS—Coats Mercerized Crochet No. 100. No. 14 Hook.

Start at one side of tab, working up and down.

Ch. 75.

1st Row—1 bl, 2 sp, 21 bl.
2nd Row—1 bl, 22 sp, 1 bl.
3rd Row—1 bl, 9 sp, 2 bl, 3 sp, 1 bl, 7 sp, 1 bl.
4th Row—Add 1 bl on lower edge, continue to follow design, adding bl to form point.

Make as many tabs as it requires to make collar the desired length.

Working Patterns for Pointed Yoke and Collar in Tabs

Edgings

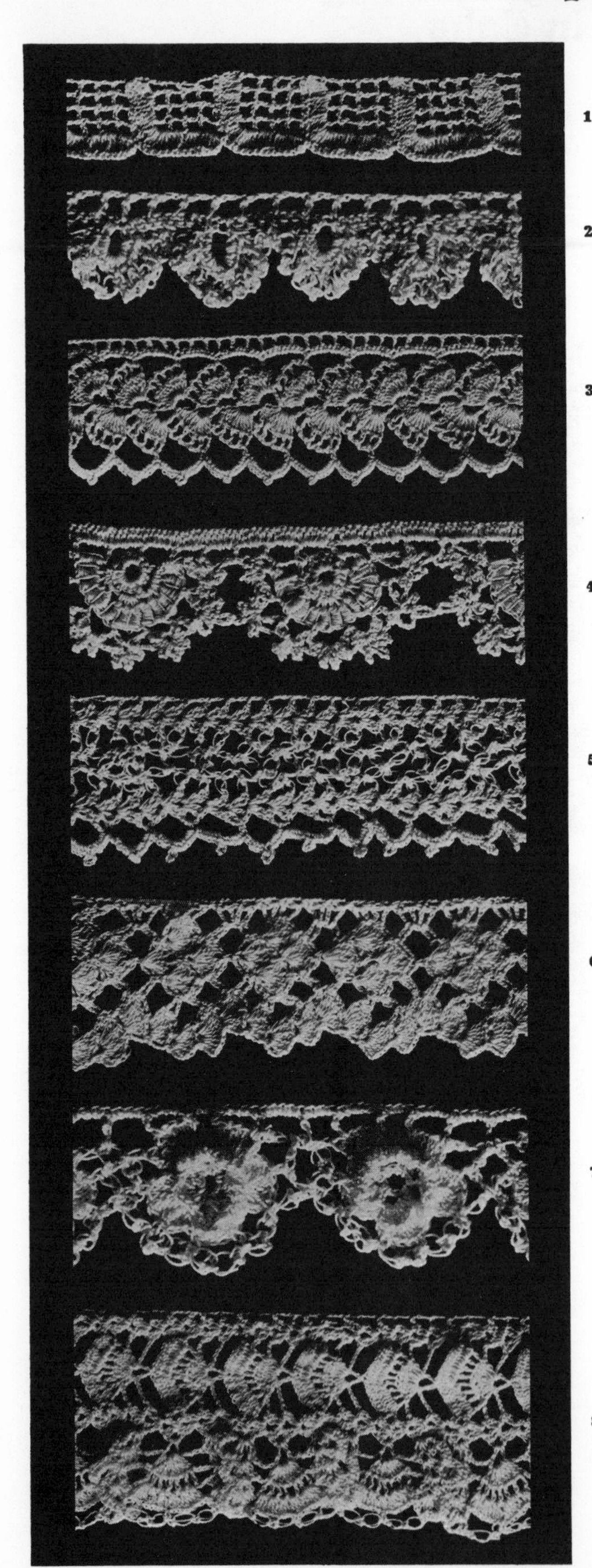
1

2

3

4

5

6

7

8

DIRECTIONS

No. 1—For the advanced worker, no directions necessary.

SINGLE ROSE EDGE

MATERIALS—No. 50 thread. No. 11 hook.

No. 2—* Ch 6, join, 15 sc in ring, turn, ch 5, * repeat desired length. For top make a row of sps, 4 sps between each ring. For lower edge, from 1st, make a short knot st. Sc into 3d in ring. Repeat around ring, 6 knot sts around ring, catching last one over the dc of 2nd sp. Repeat around all rings.

DOUBLE FAN LACE

MATERIALS—No. 70 Crochet Cotton. No. 12 hook.

No. 3—Ch 10, join. Repeat into same place. Ch 3, 10 dc over first ring. Ch 4, turn. 1 dc, 1 ch, sk 1, * repeat across. (You will have 7 dc, 6 sps). Make 2nd fan into 2nd ring same way. Ch 5, make a 3d fan in the ch between the first 2 fans, ch 5 and repeat to the desired length, turn, ch 6, sc into 1st st of next fan, repeat across, turn. Cover these ch with sc, and on the top make a row of spaces. For the lower edge, ch 12 between shs. For last row cover chs with 6 sc, p, sc.

ROLL STITCH EDGE

MATERIALS—No. 70 Crochet Cotton. No. 12 hook.

No. 4—Ch 8, join. Cover with sc. Ch 4, miss 4, sl st into 5th st, repeat 4 times.

2nd Row—Ch 3, 5 rolls st into 1st loop, 5 rolls into next loop, 5 rolls into 3d loop, turn. Ch 2, p, ch 2, sc between 2nd and 3d roll. Repeat back to 1st roll, turn. 3 loops of five ch each into 1st ch. Repeat back to last roll. Make a second scallop in same manner, on the last row, fasten the 1st of the 3 loops of 5 ch into the last one of 1st scallops. Join next center same way, fastening loops of 2nd to 6th and 1st to 7th loops. When all are done for top dc in first loop, ch 3 dc between ch and roll, ch 3 dc over ring, ch 3 dc between ch and roll, ch 3 dc between roll and loops, ch 3 dc between 2 scallops. Repeat across last row, 5 dc in each space.

KNOT STITCH

MATERIALS—No. 50 Crochet Cotton. No. 11 hook.

No. 5—Ch 20, turn. **2nd Row**—1 tr in 4th st of ch, ch 2, 2 tr in same st. 1 kt st, fasten with sc in 8th st of ch, 2 kt st, fasten with sc in 12th st of ch, 1 kt st and shell at end of ch, turn.

3rd Row—Ch 5, sh in sh, 1 kt st, fasten in kt st of 2nd row, 2 kt sts, fasten in double kt st of 2nd, fasten in double kt st of 2nd row. 1kt st and sh in sh. Ch 1, sc in 3d R L st, top of edge, turn.

4th Row—Ch 5, shell in shell, 3 kt sts, shell in shell, ch 5, turn.

For lower edge, sc in 1st sh. * Ch 12, sc in next sh, repeat from *.

2nd Row—* Sc over ch, 1 p, sc over same ch. Repeat from *.

SHELL LACE

MATERIALS—No. 50 Crochet Cotton. No. 11 hook.

No. 6—Ch 28. **1st Row**—Sc into 4th st from needle. 7 loops of 4 ch each into this ch, always fastening with a sl st, except at top, where first and last st is always a sc.

2nd Row—Ch 4, sh of 8 dc under 1st loop at lower edge, ch 8, sk 1 sl st, and fasten into next, sh in next sl st, ch 8, sk 1 sl st and sc into sc at top edge, turn.

3rd Row—Ch 4, sc into same st. Ch 4, sl st into middle of 8 ch. This makes the first of the row of loops of 4 ch each. Make 7 more loops, last one fastens to lower point of shell of bottom, turn.

4th Row—Sh under loop last made, ch 8, sk 1 sl st, fasten into sl st in middle of 8 ch, make sh in sl st at point of sh of former row. Sl st into top of sh. Sh in sl st at last point of sh, ch 4, sc into top edge, turn.

5th Row—Ch 4, sc into same place, 8 loops of 4 ch each, last one fastens into middle of lower sh, turn.

6th Row—Ch 4, sh under loop, ch 8, sl st over middle of sh of former row, sh into the sl st, between two shells, ch 8, sc into top edge, turn.

7th Row—Ch 4, sc into same st. 7 loops as in 1st row. All rows down are loops of 4 ch, shs are made in rows going up. This finishes last scallop. Repeat from 2nd row.

ROSE EDGE

MATERIALS—No. 60 Crochet Cotton. No. 12 hook.

No. 7—Make a Rose with 2 rows of leaves (5 in a row). **1st Row**—1 sc 3 dc, 1 sc, 5 times in ring.

2nd Row—1 sc, 1 dc, 6 tc, 1 dc, 1 sc, back of front row. Around lower leaves make 7 kt sts. Across two upper leaves make 3 sps. Repeat desired length.

FAN LACE

MATERIALS—No. 70 Crochet Cotton. No. 12 steel hook.

No. 8—This lace must have the upper part made the length desired, and scallops added.

Ch 16, turn. *Sh of 2 dc, 2 ch, 2 dc, in 6th st from needle. Ch 4, sk 4, dc 3 ch, dc in next, ch 4, sk 4, sh in next, ch 3, turn. Sh in sh, ch 3, 9 dc over the 3 ch, ch 3, sh in sh, dc back into point of sh of preceding row, ch 3, turn. Sh in sh, 7 dc with 1 ch between dcs in the fan, ch 3, sh in sh, ch 3, turn. Ch 1, 18 dc in fan, ch 1, sh in sh, dc, back into point of sh of former row, ch 3, turn. This finishes the scallop of top. Repeat from * for length desired.

For lower part—Sh in sh, ch 4, dc 3 ch, dc over ch of next sh, ch 4, sh in sh, ch 3, turn. Make the fan just as you did for upper row. When finished make a ch covered with sc down side of scallop, 2 half kt sts across bottom sc over ch between shs up other side of scallop. Repeat.

New Edgings

MATERIALS—Coats Mercerized Crochet, in all numbers.

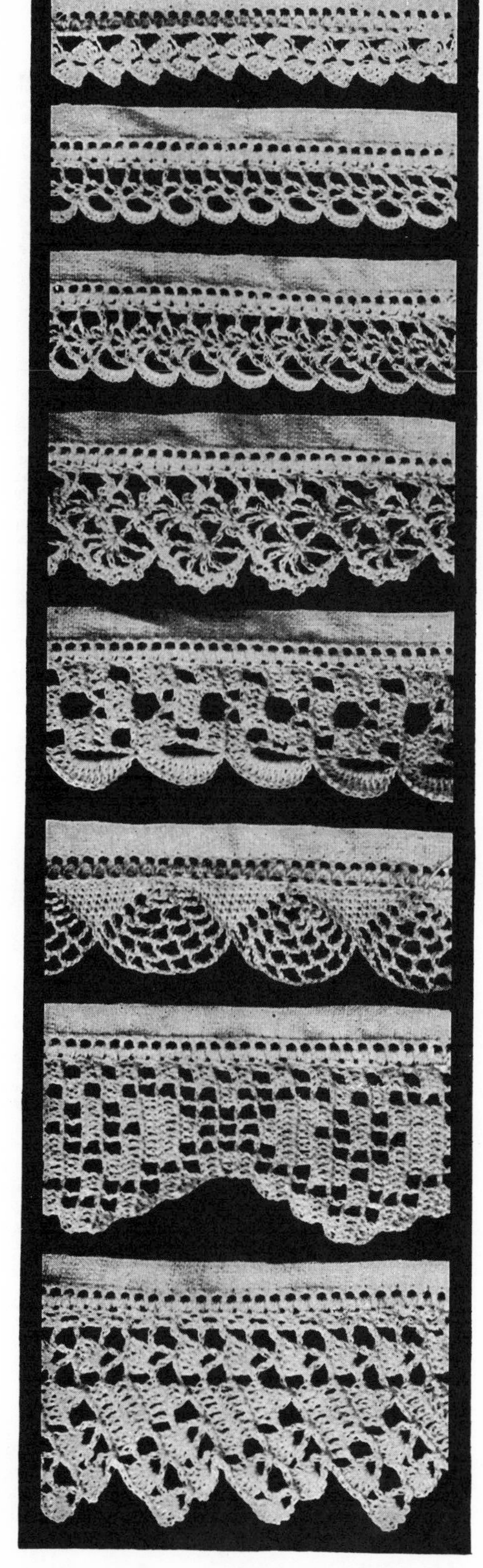

No. 1

Start at one end, working crosswise.

Ch 5, join in ring, turn, ch 3, 4 tr in ring, ch 2, 1 s st in same ring, * turn, ch 3, 4 tr in ch 2, 1 s st in same ch, repeat from *.

When the required length is made, start at one end in the outside point, * ch 5, 1 sl st in next point, repeat from *.

This last row is to make a chain to sew on to the goods.

No. 2

Start at one end, working crosswise.

Ch 9.

1st Row—1 tr in 4th st from hook, ch 2, 1 tr in same st, ch 2, 1 tr in 1st st of ch, turn.

2nd Row—Ch 5, 1 tr in ch 2, ch 2, 1 tr in same ch, ch 5, 1 sl st in end st, turn.

3rd Row—* 8s st in ch 5, ch 1, 1 tr in ch 2, ch 2, 1 tr in same ch, ch 2, 1 tr in edge, turn, ch 2, 1 tr in ch 2, ch 2, 1 tr in same ch, ch 5, 1 sl st in ch 1, turn, repeat from *.

No. 3

Start at one end, working crosswise.

Ch 9, 1 tr in 4th st from hook, ch 2, 1 tr in same st, ch 2, 1 tr in same st, ch 2, 1 tr in same st, ch 2, 1 tr in end st, turn, ch 5, * 1 tr in center ch 2, ch 2, 1 tr in same ch, ch 2, 1 tr in same st, ch 2, 1 tr in same st, ch 5, 1 sl st in end st, turn, 9 s st in ch 5, ch 2, repeat from *.

No. 4

Start at one end, working crosswise.

Ch 18, 1 d tr in 12th st from hook, ch 2, 1 d tr in same st, ch 2, 1 d tr in same st, ch 2, 1 d tr in same st, turn, * 2 s st in ch 2, ch 2, 2 s st in next ch 2, ch 2, 2 s st in next ch 2, ch 3, 1 tr in end st, turn, ch 5, 1 d tr in center ch 2, ch 2, 1 d tr in same ch, ch 2, 1 d tr in same ch, 1 d tr in end of last point (ch 2, 1 d tr in same st) 5 times, turn, 4 s st in ch 2, (1 p, 4 s st in next ch 2) 4 times, repeat from *.

No. 5

Start at one end, working crosswise.

Ch 15, 1 tr in 4th st from hook, 1 tr in each next 3 st, ch 4, 1 tr in 5th st of ch, 1 tr in each next 3 st, ch 5, turn, * 6 tr in ch 4, ch 2, 1 tr in each tr, turn, 4 tr in end sp, ch 3, 1 s st in center of 6 tr, ch 3, 4 tr in end sp, ch 8, 1 sl st in end of 1st row, turn, ch 2, 10 tr in ch 8, 1 tr in each next 4 tr, ch 4, 1 tr in each next 4 tr, ch 5, turn, repeat from *.

No. 6

Start at one end, working lengthwise.

Make a chain the length of piece desired.

1st Row—* 1 s st in each 11 st of ch, ch 2, skip 2 st of ch, repeat from *.

2nd Row—* 9 s st over 11 s st, ch 3, 1 tr in ch 2, repeat from *.

3rd Row—* 7 s st over 9 s st, ch 3, 1 tr in ch 3, ch 3, 1 tr in ch 3, ch 3, repeat from *.

4th Row—* 5 s st over 7 s st (ch 3, 1 tr in ch 3) 4 times, ch 3, repeat from *.

5th Row—* 3 s st over 5 s st (ch 3, 1 tr in ch 3) 5 times, ch 3, repeat from *.

6th Row—* 1 s st over 3 s st (ch 3, 1 tr in ch 3) 6 times, ch 3, repeat from *.

No. 7

Start at one end, working crosswise.

Ch 21.

1st Row—1 bl, 3 sp, 1 bl, 1 sp.

2nd Row—1 bl, 4 sp, 1 bl.

3rd Row—Add block at lower edge, continue to follow design.

No. 8

Start at one end, working crosswise.

Ch 22, 1 tr in 5th st from hook, ch 2, 1 tr in 3rd st, ch 2, 1 tr in same st, ch 2, 3 tr in 3rd st, ch 2, 1 tr in 5th st, ch 2, 1 tr in same st, ch 2, 1 tr in 5th st, ch 2, 1 tr in same st, turn, * ch 3, 4 tr in ch 2, 5 tr in next ch 2, ch 2, 1 tr in ch 2, 1 tr in each next 3 tr, 1 tr in ch 2, ch 2, 5 tr in ch 2, ch 2, 2 tr in end ch 2, turn, ch 3, 1 tr in next tr, ch 2, 1 tr in center of 5 tr, ch 2, 1 tr in same st, ch 2, 1 tr in ch 2, 1 tr in each next 5 tr, 1 tr in ch 2, ch 2, 1 tr in center of 5 tr, ch 2, 1 tr in same st, ch 2, 1 tr in center of next 5 tr, ch 2, 1 tr in same st, turn, ch 3, 1 tr in ch 2, 5 tr in next ch 2, ch 2, 1 tr in ch 2, 1 tr in each next 7 tr, 1 tr in ch 2, ch 2, 5 tr in ch 2, ch 2, 2 tr in end tr, turn, ch 3, 1 tr in next tr, ch 2, 1 tr in center of 5 tr, ch 2, 1 tr in same st, ch 2, 3 tr in 1st tr of next group, ch 2, 1 tr in 4th tr of same group, ch 2, 1 tr in same st, ch 2, 1 tr in last tr of same group, ch 2, 1 tr in same st, turn, repeat from *.

New Edgings

MATERIALS—Coats Mercerized Crochet in all numbers.

No. 1

Start at one end, working lengthwise.

* ch 6, 1 sl st in 3rd st from hook, 3 tr in same st, ch 3, 1 sl st in same st, repeat from *.

No. 2

Start at one end, working crosswise.

Ch 18, 1 tr in 3rd st from 1st end, 1 tr in 1st end st, ch 3, turn, * 1 tr in 3rd st before the last tr, turn, ch 7, 1 sl st in end st, 9 s st in ch 7, 3 s st around last tr, 3 s st in next ch, ch 8, 1 tr in 3rd s st, 1 tr in next 3rd s st, ch 3, repeat from *.

No. 3

Start at one end, working lengthwise.

Make chain the length of piece desired.

1st Row—Sp whole length.

2nd Row—Start in tr, * ch 4, 3 h d tr in 2nd sp, ch 2, 3 h d tr in same sp, ch 4, 1 sl st in 2nd tr, turn, 5 s st in ch 4, 2 s st in ch 2, 1 p, 2 s st in same ch, 5 s st in ch 4, sl st across sp to next tr, repeat from *.

No. 4

Start at one end, working lengthwise.

Make a chain the length of piece desired.

1st Row—Sp whole length.

2nd Row—Start in sp, * ch 3, 1 tr in same sp, ch 4, 1 sl st in 2nd sp, ch 4, 1 tr in 2nd sp, repeat from *.

3rd Row—Start in ch 3, * 7 tr in same ch, 1 s st in same ch, ch 5, 1 s st in next ch 3, repeat from *.

No. 5

Start at one end, working crosswise.

Ch 14, 1 tr in 11th st from hook, ch 2, 1 tr in same st, * ch 4, turn, 1 tr in ch 2, ch 2, 1 tr in same ch, ch 5, turn, 1 tr in ch 2, 1 tr in same ch, ch 2, 5 tr in ch 4, ch 2, 5 tr in same ch, 1 s st in end st, turn, ch 6, 1 s st in ch 2 (ch 3, 1 s st in same ch) 3 times, ch 6, 1 s st in ch 2, ch 2, 1 tr in ch 2 ch 2, 1 tr in same chain, repeat from *.

When piece is the length desired, make a chain along upper edge to sew to goods as follows: Start in point at upper edge, * ch 5, 1 s st in next point, repeat from *.

No. 6

Start at one end, working lengthwise.

Make a chain the length desired.

1st Row—Sp the entire length.

2nd Row—Start in sp, ch 5, 1 s st in next sp, * ch 3, 1 tr in 2nd sp, ch 4, 1 tr in same sp, ch 3, 1 s st in 2nd sp, repeat from *.

3rd Row—Start in s st, * ch 3, 3 tr in ch 4, ch 2, 3 tr in same ch, ch 2, 3 tr in same ch, ch 3, 1 s st in s st, repeat from *

4th Row—* 1 pc st in 2nd tr, ch 3, 1 pc st in ch 2, ch 3, 1 pc st in 2nd tr, ch 3, 1 pc st in ch 2, ch 3, 1 pc st in 2nd tr, repeat from *.

5th Row—* 2 s st in ch 2, 1 p, 2 s st in same ch, repeat from *.

Use Popcorn Stitch (pc st), see head of this page

No. 7

Start at one end, working lengthwise.

Make a chain the length of piece desired.

1st Row—Sp entire length.

2nd Row—Start in tr, * ch 12, 1 s st in 2nd tr, turn, 14 s st in ch 12, turn, 1 s st in each of the 14 s st, turn, ch 5, 1 tr in 1st s st (ch 2, 1 tr in 2nd s st, 1 tr in next s st) 4 times, turn, (1 s st in each 2 tr, 2 s st in ch 2, 1 p, 2 s st in same ch) 5 times, ch 3, 1 s st in next tr of 1st row, 3 s st in next sp, 1 s st in next tr, repeat from *.

No. 8

Start at one end, working lengthwise.

Make a chain length of piece desired.

1st Row—Sp entire length.

2nd Row—Start in sp, * ch 4, 1 tr in 2nd sp, ch 3, 1 tr in same sp, ch 4, 1 s st in 2nd sp, repeat from *.

3rd Row—* 1 pc st in ch 3, ch 4, 1 pc st in same ch, ch 5, repeat from *.

4th Row—* 1 pc st in ch 4, ch 5, 1 pc st in same ch, ch 3, 1 s st in ch 5, ch 3, repeat from *.

5th Row—* 10 s st in ch 5, ch 4, repeat from *.

Use Popcorn Stitch (pc st), see head of this page.

No. 9—Pointed Edge

Start at top, working lengthwise.

Make chain as long as edge is desired, make sp entire length.

POINT—Start in 5th tr, ch 12, 1 sl st in 2nd tr, ch 12, 1 sl st in 2nd tr, ch 12, 1 sl st in 2nd tr, turn, 15 s st in ch 12, 1 sl st in sl st, 15 s st in ch 12, 1 sl st in sl st, 8 s st in 1st half of ch 12, turn, ch 12, 1 sl st in center of 15 s st, ch 12, 1 sl st in center of next 15 s st, turn, 15 s st in ch 12, 1 sl st in sl st, 8 s st in 1st half of ch 12, turn, ch 12, 1 sl st in center of 15 s st, turn, 15 s st in ch 12, 8 s st in next half of ch 12, 8 s st in next half of ch 12, sl st to next tr of 1st row, turn, (ch 5, 1 sl st in 3rd s st) 11 times, ch 5, 1 s st in next tr of 1st row, sl st to next tr of 1st row, turn, * ch 5, 1 sl st in center of ch 5 of last row, * repeat all around, 1 sl st in next tr of 1st row, turn, * ch 8, 1 sl st in center of 2nd ch 5, repeat from last *, all around, turn, (10 s st in ch 8) 4 times, 5 s st in 1st half of next ch 8, turn, ch 8, 1 sl st in center of last 10 s st, turn, 10 s st in last ch 8, 4 s st in half of ch 8 (10 s st in ch 8) 3 times, this completes one point.

POP CORN STITCH (pc st)

Have st on hook, thread over, insert hook, pull through, thread over, insert hook in same place, pull through, thread over, insert hook in same place, pull through; thread over, insert hook in same place, pull through; there should now be 10 stitches on hook, thread over, pull through all the 10 stitches at once.

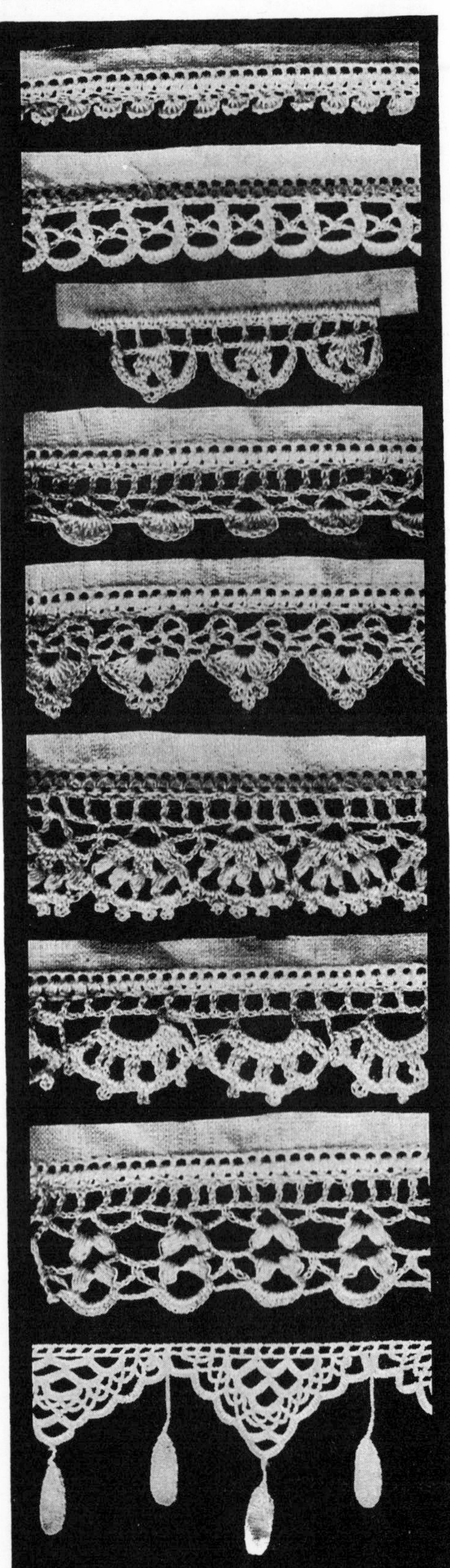

New Edgings

NOTE

If the edge is machine-hemstitched, crochet in each stitch of the hemstitching with 1 s st. When a pattern is made lengthwise, it may be crocheted into this instead of making a chain .

MATERIALS—Coats Mercerized Crochet in all numbers.

No. 1

Start at one end, working lengthwise.
Make a chain the length required.
1st Row—Sp whole length.
2nd Row—Like 1st row.
3rd Row—Start in sp, * ch 7 in next sp, 2 s st in next sp, 2 s st in next sp, repeat from *.
4th Row—1 s st in each of the 7 tr, * ch 6, 1 s st in each of the next 7 tr, repeat from *.

No. 2

Start at one end, working lengthwise.
Make a chain the length of strip desired.
1st Row—Sp whole length.
2nd Row—* 1 sp, 1 bl, repeat from *.
3rd Row—Start in sp, * ch 5, 3 s st in next sp, repeat from *.
4th Row—* 8 s st in ch 5, 1 s st in center of 3 s st, repeat from *.

No. 3

Start at one end, working crosswise.
Ch 12, join in ring, * 8 s st in ring, turn, ch 6, 1 d tr in 1st s st (ch 2, 1 d tr in next s st) 6 times, turn, (1 s st in d tr, 2 s st in ch 2) 7 times, turn, ch 12, 1 sl st in 3rd s st, turn, repeat from *.

No. 4

Start at one end, working lengthwise.
Make a chain the required length.
1st Row—Sp all the length.
2nd Row—Start in tr, * ch 10, 1 sl st in 2nd tr, ch 2, 1 sl st in next tr, turn, 12 tr in ch 10, turn, 1 s st in each 1st 3 tr, 1 p, 1 s st in each next 3 tr, 1 p, 1 s st in each next 3 tr, 1 p, 1 s st in each next 3 tr, repeat from *.

No. 5

Make the discs first, as follows: Start in center, ch 10, join in ring, 15 s st in ring, continue to work around until 4 rows of s st are made, adding stitches often enough to make it lay flat, make all the discs and sew together.

UPPER EDGE—Make * 3 tr on top of disc, with a ch of 2 between each 2 tr, ch 2, 1 d tr where two discs join; repeat from *.

LOWER EDGE—Start where 2 discs join, ch 7, * 1 tr one-third the way across disc, ch 5, 1 tr one-third the way across the same disc, ch 3, 1 tr where the 2 discs join, ch 3, repeat from *.

2nd Row—Start in the tr between the discs, * ch 5, 4 tr in ch 5, ch 3, 4 tr in same ch, ch 5, 1 sl st in tr between discs, repeat from *.

3rd Row—* 1 s st in each of the 4 tr, 5 s st in ch 3, 1 s st in each of the next 4 tr, ch 4, repeat from *.

No. 6

Make the round disc first, as follows: Start in center, ch 6, join in ring, make 8 s st in ring.

2nd Row—Make 1 s st in each s st, 1 s st after each 4 st, or often enough so they will lay flat.

Make 4 times around, break cotton, sew discs together as shown in design.
Top is worked lengthwise like sp.
2nd row of top, sp whole length.

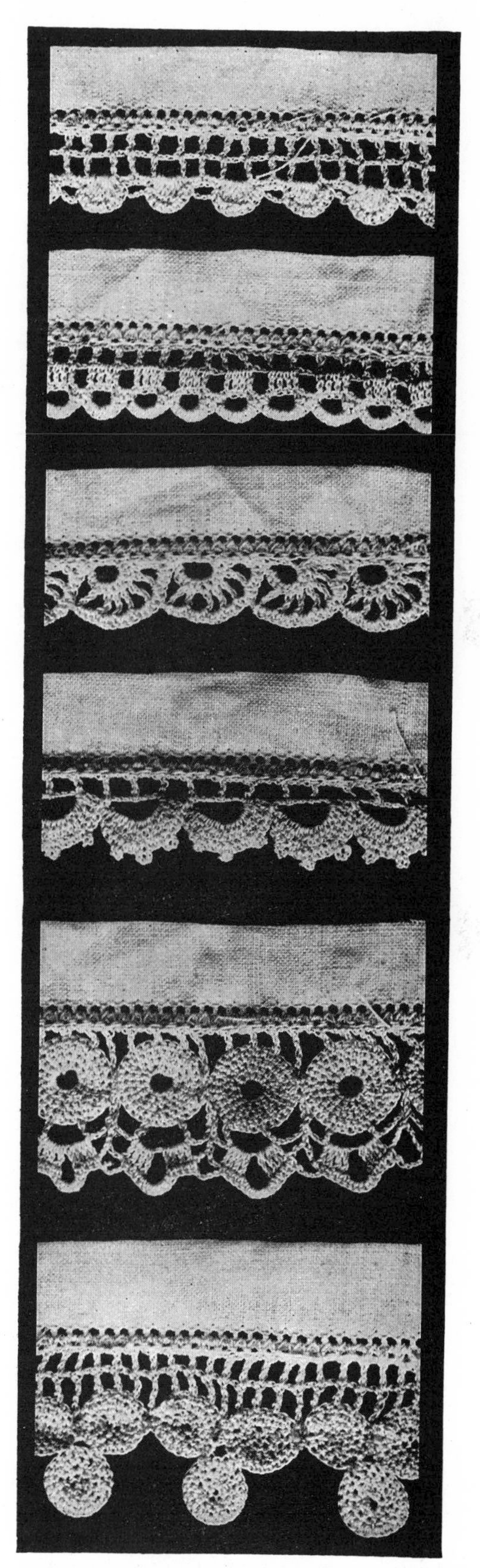

DOVER BOOKS ON QUILTING, CROCHET, KNITTING AND OTHER AREAS

NATURAL DYES AND HOME DYEING, Rita J. Adrosko. (22688-3) $2.25

APPLIQUÉ OLD AND NEW, Nedda C. Anders. (23246-8) $2.75

THE UNITED STATES PATCHWORK PATTERN BOOK, Barbara Bannister and Edna P. Ford. (23243-3) $2.75

STATE CAPITALS QUILT BLOCKS, Barbara Bannister and Edna Paris Ford (eds.). (23557-2) $2.50

BRAIDING AND KNOTTING, Constantine A. Belash. (23059-7) $2.00

ENCYLOPEDIA OF VICTORIAN NEEDLEWORK, S.F.A. Caulfeild and Blanche C. Saward. (22800-2, 22801-0) Two-volume set $12.00

THE COMPLETE BOOK OF DOLL MAKING AND COLLECTING, Catherine Christopher. (22066-4) $4.50

DESIGN AND MAKE YOUR OWN FLORAL APPLIQUÉ, Eva Costabel-Deutsch. (23427-4) $2.50

KNIT YOUR OWN NORWEGIAN SWEATERS, Dale Yarn Company. (23031-7) $3.25

EASY-TO-MAKE FELT ORNAMENTS, Betty Deems. (23389-8) $3.00

SMOCKING: TECHNIQUES, PROJECTS AND DESIGNS, Dianne Durand. (23788-5) $2.00

EASY-TO-MAKE BEAN BAG TOYS, Jane Ethe. (23884-9) $2.50

EASY AND ATTRACTIVE GIFTS YOU CAN SEW, Jane Ethe and Josephine Kirshon. (23638-2) $3.50

EARLY AMERICAN PATCHWORK PATTERNS, Carol Belanger Grafton. (23882-2) $3.00

GEOMETRIC PATCHWORK PATTERNS, Carol Belanger Grafton. (23183-6) $3.00

TRADITIONAL PATCHWORK PATTERNS, Carol Belanger Grafton. (23015-5) $3.00

PATCHWORK PLAYTHINGS WITH FULL-SIZE TEMPLATES, Margaret Hutchings. (23247-6) $2.00

TEDDY BEARS AND HOW TO MAKE THEM, Margaret Hutchings. (23487-8) $5.95

THE STANDARD BOOK OF QUILT MAKING AND COLLECTING, Marguerite Ickis. (20582-7) $4.95

EASY-TO-MAKE DOLLS WITH NINETEENTH-CENTURY COSTUMES, G.P. Jones. (23426-6) $2.95

FILET CROCHET: PROJECTS AND DESIGNS, Mrs. F. W. Kettelle. (23745-1) $1.75

FIRST BOOK OF MODERN LACE KNITTING, Marianne Kinzel. (22904-1) $3.50